The Old Port of MONTRÉAL

Collaboration, texts: Annick Poussart

Verification of historical content: Paul-André Linteau

Design and computer graphics: Patrice St-Amour

Image processing, obtaining permissions for illustrations
and credit compilation: Mélanie Sabourin

Correction: Brigitte Lépine

Technical support: Mario Paquin

Old Port of Montréal Corporation
Communications Director: Lily Robert

Cover page photo
Benoit Chalifour

Photo credits - fourth cover page

Above left: *Harbour from Custom House, Montreal, QC, 1887-88,*
Wm. Notman & Son, 1887-1888, 19th century, VIEW-1940
© McCord Museum

Above right: Olivier Hanigan

Below left: Library and Archives Canada

Below centre: Archives of the Port of Montréal

Below right: *Highwater, Montreal harbour, QC, about 1870*
Alexander Henderson, about 1870, 19th century,
MP-0000.1452.41 © McCord Museum

Bibliothèque et Archives nationales du Québec and Library and
Archives Canada cataloguing in publication

Desjardins, Pauline

    The Old Port of Montréal

    Translation of: Le Vieux-Port de Montréal

    1. Vieux-Port (Montréal, Québec) - Pictorial works.
    2. Vieux-Port (Montréal, Québec) - History. I. Title.

    FC2947.55.D47213 2007   971.14'2800222   C2006-941747-4

For more information about our publications,
please visit our website: www.edhomme.com
Other sites of interest: www.edjour.com
www.edtypo.com • www.edvlb.com
www.edhexagone.com • www.edutilis.com

Version française disponible

07-07

© 2007, Les Éditions de l'Homme,
a division of the Sogides Group Inc., a subsidiary
of Quebecor Media Book Group Inc.
(Montréal, Quebec)

Legal deposit: 2007
Bibliothèque et Archives nationales du Québec

ISBN 978-2-7619-2231-9

EXCLUSIVE DISTRIBUTORS:

• For Canada
  and the United States:

MESSAGERIES ADP*

2315, rue de la Province

Longueuil, Quebec J4G 1G4

Tel.: 450 640-1237

Fax: 450 674-6237

* a division of the Sogides Group Inc.,
  a subsidiary of Quebecor Media Book Group Inc.

• For France and other countries:

INTERFORUM

Immeuble Paryseine,
3 Allée de la Seine

94854 Ivry Cedex

Tél.: 01 49 59 11 89/91

Fax: 01 49 59 11 33

Orders: Tél.: 02 38 32 71 00

            Fax: 02 38 32 71 28

• For Switzerland:

INTERFORUM SWITZERLAND

P.O. Box 69 - 1701 Fribourg - Switzerland

Tél.: (41-26) 460-80-60

Fax: (41-26) 460-80-68

Internet: www.havas.ch

E-mail: office@havas.ch

Distribution: OLF SA

Z.I. 3, Corminbœuf

P.O. Box 1061

CH-1701 Fribourg

Orders: Tél.: (41-26) 467-53-33

            Fax: (41-26) 467-54-66

• For Belgium and Luxembourg:

INTERFORUM

Boulevard de l'Europe 117

B-1301 Wavre

Tél.: (010) 42-03-20

Fax: (010) 41-20-24

Government of Québec - Tax credit for book
publishing – Administered by SODEC – www.sodec.
gouv.qc.ca

The publisher gratefully acknowledges the support of
the Société de développement des entreprises
culturelles du Québec for its publishing program.

Le Conseil des Arts du Canada
The Canada Council for the Arts

We gratefully acknowledge the support of the Canada
Council for the Arts for its publishing program.

We acknowledge the financial support of the
Government of Canada through the Book Publishing
Industry Development Program (BPIDP) for our
publishing activities.

Pauline Desjardins

The Old Port of Montréal

Translated from the French
by Barbara Sandilands

OLD PORT
OF MONTRÉAL
CORPORATION

Canadä

LES ÉDITIONS DE
L'HOMME

Dropping anchor

From the port to the Old Port: A few recollections

Nowadays, the Port of Montréal, with its freighters, landing stages, warehouses, grain elevators and trains, stretches for tens of kilometres along the magnificent St. Lawrence River. But, in the heart of this hustle and bustle, the oldest part of the port still lies, fragile and sensitive, as if nestled in the arms of one of the largest commercial ports in North America.

Since 1981, the words "meetings", "coming alongside", and " outward bound" have taken on new meaning: the waterfront strip formerly restricted to captains, sailors and longshoremen is now accessible to everyone, as the "Old Port of Montréal".

The transformation began toward the end of the 1960s. The Montréal port authorities were resolved to renovate the facilities, which were in a very bad state of repair, to make them fit for container handling. This decision was in line with an international movement in the second half of the twentieth century that affected large ports the world over. By renewing their facilities, ports were attempting to retain their influence.

A number of projects were carried out with this goal in mind. Several sheds were demolished, as was the largest portion of the flood wall that had been built at the beginning of the twentieth century between Bonsecours and McGill streets. Bonsecours Basin was filled in so that a container terminal could be built. Gradually, transhipping activities shifted to the east and west, leaving the original site in a state of neglect and breaking the centuries-old link between the city and the river. What's more, Montréal's downtown had already shifted north, draining the historic district of its vitality.

A few years later, in December 1977, the federal government, owner of the harbourfront, announced that it would build its container terminal further east. This meant that the areas going to waste along the river could be used for a major urban redevelopment project, as was already being done in several large cities around the world.

In the spring of 1978, a group of Montréal residents formed the Association/Le Vieux-Port to exert influence over the kinds of changes being proposed, reflecting the evergrowing importance of heritage conservation and development to a population concerned with preserving its identity. In June 1978, the government decided to hold a public consultation on the future of the Old Port, and the job of coordinating it was given to the Association. However, a year before the consultation ended, elevator 2, located across from Bonsecours Market, was demolished. This caused a general outcry and led the Association to make a number of recommendations the following year. For example, the redevelopment of the site would have to act as a catalyst for the revitalisation of Old Montréal and stimulate Montrealers' interest in the old district, and the preservation of heritage structures would form the backdrop for all development projects. In particular, the superb "sea front" along De la Commune Street would have to be protected.

In 1981, the government decided to invest in a first phase of development. On November 26, it established the Canada Lands Company (Old Port of Montréal) Limited, now the Old Port of Montréal Corporation Inc., with the following objectives: to protect and promote an important piece of Canada's cultural heritage; to improve urban living conditions; to give the public easier access to the river; to contribute to regional economic development; to maintain port operations in an urban and historic setting; and to showcase the federal government's dynamic presence on the site.

Two months later, the Corporation signed a management agreement with the Department of Public Works and Government Services to develop, lay out and bring to life "a window on the river, a riverside park on the Old Port of Montréal site", a strip of 53 hectares corresponding to the oldest part of the port. It thus became the manager of Clock Tower Quay (formerly Victoria pier), Jacques Cartier Quay and King Edward Quay, the downstream entrance of the Lachine Canal and the park at the tip of Cité-du-Havre.

Between 1981 and 1984, elevator 1 was demolished to create an even wider window on the river, but the elevator's footprint would live on in the long basin dug in its place. The reinforcement of the quays was begun, as were the first repairs to the Clock Tower. Then the police station and the cold storage warehouse were gutted, with the intention of eventually restoring them. It was during this period that some of the old sheds were torn down, but sheds 3 to 6 on Alexandra Quay, 7 to 10 on King Edward Quay, and shed 16 on Clock Tower Quay were preserved. The downstream entrance to the Lachine Canal (locks 1 and 2), which had been filled in after the Seaway was opened, was cleared out.

At the end of 1984, however, the prospect of real estate development on the newly cleared land caused a controversy. A second public consultation was therefore carried out, resulting in a clear message: residential development, intensive commercial development and heavy industrial port activities must be ruled out for good. The Old Port would provide leisure space for the public and would become a cultural destination, part of the development of recreational and tourist facilities in an urban setting. Its redevelopment projects would reflect the maritime and historic character of the site, highlight archaeological remains and be an integral part of the renaissance of Old Montréal and the downtown core. Development would take place in stages, and new additions would blend in harmoniously with what had previously been done.

To follow up on the consultation, a vision statement and a development plan were tabled in 1987. Strict principles for development were then set out, including respect for the integrity of the site, the reversibility of any intervention, the conservation of heritage elements to preserve the unity of the site, the re-use of the facilities and historical interpretation.

Once again the federal government invested considerable amounts so that a second phase of development could be carried out. To the west, the Lachine Canal and the gates of locks 1 and 2 were refurbished, opening up the site for sailing and for the enjoyment of exceptional views of its industrial heritage. The eastern sector was transformed as well, making way for Bonsecours Basin, with its welcoming pavilion and outdoor skating rink. Jacques Cartier Quay was developed so that it could host large-scale events, and its pavilion has become a summer destination that is not to be missed. While yachts and sailboats drop anchor in the marina, cruise boats dock along the quays, providing access to everything the river has to offer and to new views of the city.

On this new playing field, the Old Port Corporation wanted to encourage artists and innovators to express themselves through rich and varied programming. It scheduled interactive events. It launched the first of nine editions of Expotec, a large public exhibition dedicated to science and technology. Shortly thereafter, it opened an IMAX theatre that even today is one of the most popular in North America. So it was that the Old Port became the favourite destination for Montrealers and tourists. It is no longer a port for goods in transit; instead, it has become an urban cultural crossroads where ideas, experiences, and emotions are shared, Canada Day is celebrated, the artistic initiatives of Robert Lepage or the premieres of Cirque du Soleil are performed . . .

All of these projects, inaugurated in 1992 on the 350th anniversary of the founding of Montréal, soon earned the Old Port many awards from national and international organizations, in fields as varied as architecture, historical conservation, maritime restoration, urban planning, landscape architecture and

tourism. But the most important reward came from the public itself: in the very first year, more than five million visitors swarmed to the Old Port, exceeding the annual total of three million visitors that had been predicted.

Encouraged by this enthusiastic reception, the Corporation undertook the development of the central portion of the site in 1997. With new federal government investment and thanks to the support of large Canadian businesses, a third phase of development was begun. This time, the plan was to transform the sheds on King Edward Quay into a destination offering educational leisure pastimes and stimulating knowledge-based activities for young people and families. In 2000, the Montréal Science Centre was opened. This institution, which had been germinating in Quebec for over twenty years, succeeded in getting industry involved with a project of social value and interesting it in the future development of science and technology, continuing education for teachers, the promotion of Canadian innovations and the growth of a socially aware scientific culture. Again, this was a huge success: now more than seven million people, mainly from the greater Montréal area, come to participate in interactive and live exhibitions, cultural and educational activities and a movie game. For some, the Old Port has become a place to come back to over and over again, to relax, participate in large-scale events, enjoy an endless series of new experiences and appreciate what makes our city so special.

Today, twenty-five years after it was established, the Old Port of Montréal Corporation, through this book, is taking another vital step forward in the development of the site. For this centuries-old harbour, rich in history and memories, has many stories to tell.

We asked Pauline Desjardins, an archaeologist and specialist in industrial heritage, to orchestrate the exploration of this exceptional site. Rather than following a strictly chronological path, she has chosen to let us discover the site through its characteristic features: its heritage, its activities, its maritime ties. Thus, from chapter to chapter, and as a result of detailed research in documentary and iconographic archives, she brings together the landscapes of yesterday and today, creating striking images of change and giving meaning to a thousand and one details. We discover the extent of the harbour's impact on the development of Montréal, Canada, and all of North America. We realize that the site has long been a meeting place for Montrealers. We find ourselves imagining voices, faces and gestures, and we too want to climb aboard.

I want to thank the author for having so successfully communicated the very essence of the Old Port. And I hope that this work will in turn help the reader to understand the road we have travelled and to imagine with us the possibilities that lie ahead.

Claude Benoit
President of the Old Port
of Montréal Corporation
Montréal, September 2007

To all those who built the Port of Montréal,

whose names are lost to history

but whose memory lingers in the air,

earth and water of the Old Port

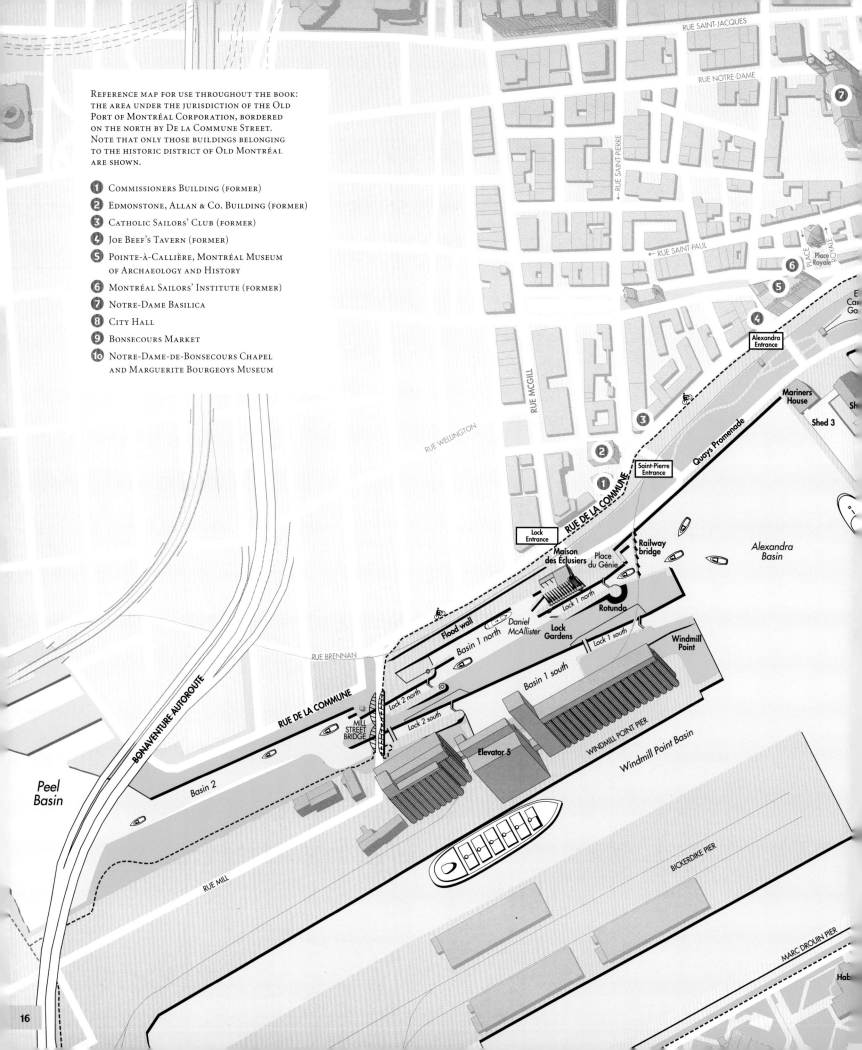

Reference map for use throughout the book: the area under the jurisdiction of the Old Port of Montréal Corporation, bordered on the north by De la Commune Street. Note that only those buildings belonging to the historic district of Old Montréal are shown.

1 Commissioners Building (former)

2 Edmonstone, Allan & Co. Building (former)

3 Catholic Sailors' Club (former)

4 Joe Beef's Tavern (former)

5 Pointe-à-Callière, Montréal Museum of Archaeology and History

6 Montréal Sailors' Institute (former)

7 Notre-Dame Basilica

8 City Hall

9 Bonsecours Market

10 Notre-Dame-de-Bonsecours Chapel and Marguerite Bourgeoys Museum

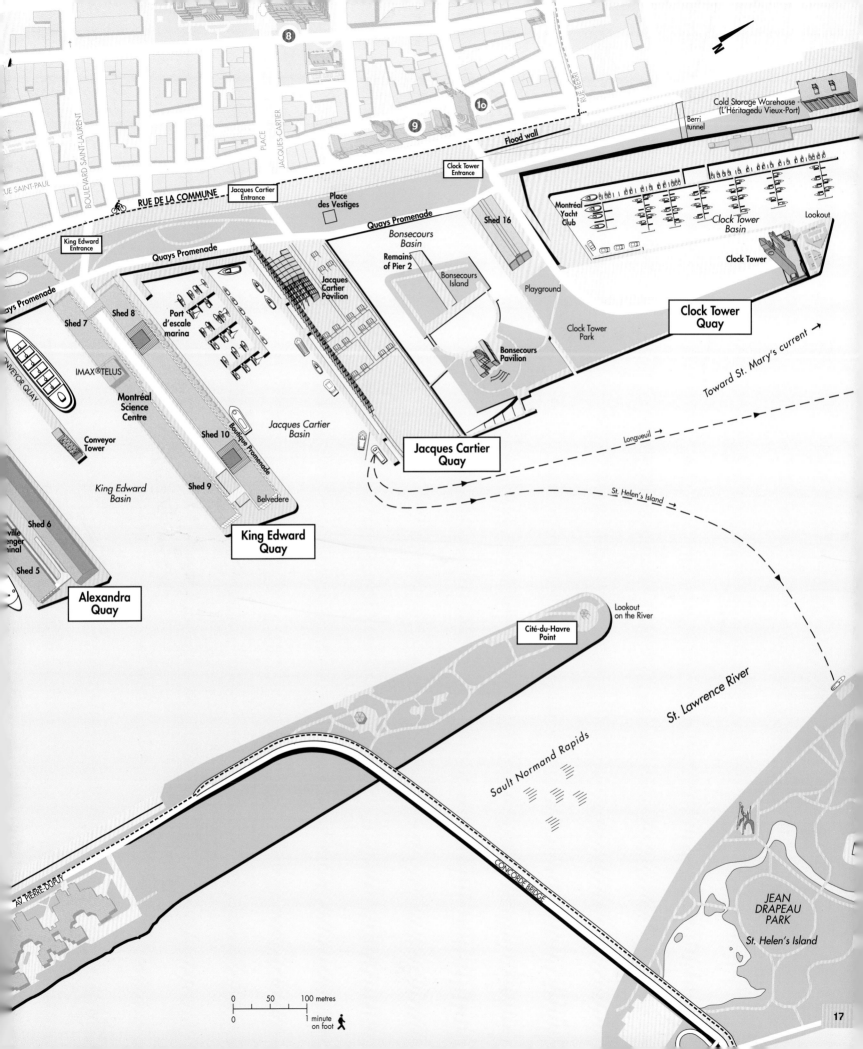

RUE SAINT-PAUL

BOULEVARD SAINT-LAURENT

PLACE JACQUES-CARTIER

RUE BERRI

⑧

⑨

⑩

Cold Storage Warehouse
(L'Héritage du Vieux-Port)

Berri
tunnel

Flood wall

RUE DE LA COMMUNE

Jacques Cartier
Entrance

Clock Tower
Entrance

Place
des Vestiges

King Edward
Entrance

Quays Promenade

Quays Promenade

Quays Promenade

Shed 16

Montréal Yacht
Club

Clock Tower
Basin

Lookout

Bonsecours
Basin

Clock Tower

Jacques
Cartier
Pavilion

Remains
of Pier 2

Bonsecours Island

Clock Tower
Quay

Shed 7

Shed 8

Port
d'escale
marina

Playground

CONVEYOR QUAY

IMAX®TELUS

Montréal
Science
Centre

Jacques Cartier
Basin

Bonsecours
Pavilion

Clock Tower
Park

Toward St. Mary's current

Conveyor
Tower

Shed 10

Boutique Promenade

Jacques Cartier
Quay

Longueuil →

King Edward
Basin

Shed 9

Belvedere

King Edward
Quay

St. Helen's Island →

Shed 6

Shed 5

ville
enger
inal

Alexandra
Quay

Lookout
on the River

Cité-du-Havre
Point

St. Lawrence River

AV. PIERRE-DUPUY

Sault Normand Rapids

CONCORDE BRIDGE

JEAN
DRAPEAU
PARK

St. Helen's Island

0   50   100 metres
0
                    1 minute
                    on foot

A past stirring all around us

Take a stroll around the Old Port of Montréal and you will soon notice traces of a busy industrial past—metal or concrete structures, whose very existence raises questions. In the past, there were those who said they should be torn down. Today, the very distinctive look of these architectural structures inspires television and film producers, who gladly use them as a backdrop or to make memories for the future. But even more importantly, in addition to being picturesque, the grain elevators, sheds and quays of the Old Port, as well as the splendid row of buildings running along De la Commune Street, have many tales to tell of a natural harbour, whose remarkable destiny it was to become one of the great seaports of the Americas. Let's take a closer look at what they have to say.

PRECEDING PAGES
THE ENTRANCE TO THE
OLD PORT OF MONTRÉAL,
AS SEEN BY NAVIGATORS
ARRIVING FROM THE EAST.

ON THE LEFT
THIS UNUSUAL VIEW
OF THE OLD PORT WITH,
IN THE FOREGROUND,
THE ROOF OF NOTRE DAME
BASILICA, FROM WHERE
THE PHOTO WAS TAKEN,
SHOWS THE CONVEYOR
TOWER (A "MARINE TOWER")
STANDING AT THE END
OF THE QUAY OF THE SAME
NAME. THIS CURIOUS
STRUCTURE, WHOSE
OPERATION IS DESCRIBED
LATER IN THE BOOK,
DATES FROM THE TIME
WHEN THIS WAS A
GRAIN HANDLING PORT.

A unique heritage

1 Elevator 1

2 Elevator 2

3 Sheds

4 Marine towers of elevator 1 (one of which remains)

5 Marine tower of elevator 2 (whose foundations can still be seen in Bonsecours Basin)

6 Overhead conveyor galleries

So much has changed since this relatively recent photo was taken! In 1962, the site still had all the facilities of an international grain port, including elevators, marine towers and overhead conveyor galleries for transshipping grain, and rows of sheds used by shipping companies. But with the completion of the St. Lawrence Seaway in 1959 and as the functions of the port changed, it became necessary to modernize the facilities.

1962

Old Port of Montréal

St. Lawrence Boulevard National Historic Site

Historic district of Old Montréal

Lachine Canal National Historic Site of Canada

Montréal's birthplace

A grain-handling system, railway lines, locks . . . The Old Port of Montréal is home to an architectural heritage that can only be described as exceptional, the legacy of its rich past as a harbour.

Of course, time has taken its toll. Many of the facilities, most of which were built between 1830 and 1925, have been torn down or altered. Others lie under the grass, trees or asphalt—sometimes several metres below the surface: the first wooden quays, the stone revetment wall, the foundations of long-gone elevators. But some can still be seen, including the concrete quays, the locks and some of the storage sheds, as well as facilities built in recent decades.

The landscape of the Old Port encompasses and preserves a unique historical, industrial and maritime heritage, where the innovative spirit that inspired the builders is particularly obvious. The hard work involved in *transshipping* (the transfer of goods from one means of transport to another—from train to boat, and from boat to boat . . .) and the handling that took place everywhere in the port led those in charge to use energy sources, transportation systems, and construction materials and techniques that were revolutionary in their day, all of which contributed to the country's economic development and growth.

In 1997, the Government of Quebec recognized that the port's heritage should be preserved for the public. As a result the limits of the historic district of Old Montréal were expanded to include almost all of the site. As well, three buildings were given special heritage status, as described in the following pages.

A site rich in history

Intrinsic aesthetic value is no longer the only criterion for listing a building as an historic monument. Three of the Old Port's buildings—elevator 5, the cold storage warehouse and the Clock Tower—are now designated as federal heritage buildings. When these works of architecture and engineering were evaluated using artistic, technological, social and symbolic criteria, the obvious conclusion was that they had played a very significant role in the history of the Old Port.

Similarly, the buildings in cut stone overlooking the Old Port along De la Commune Street are not just examples of beautiful architecture: they are reminders of the role their owners played in the economic and social development of Montréal and of the country as a whole.

BEHIND ELEVATOR 5,
THE OUTLINES OF VICTORIA
BRIDGE AND CHAMPLAIN
BRIDGE ARE VISIBLE.
IN THE FOREGROUND
IS POINTE-À-CALLIÈRE,
THE MONTRÉAL MUSEUM
OF ARCHAEOLOGY AND
HISTORY, WHERE TRACES
OF THE CITY'S FOUNDING
SITE CAN BE SEEN.

The expansion of the port through the centuries

The structural heritage preserved in the Old Port of Montréal also bears witness to the continual changes made to the port to meet the ever-growing needs of the Canadian population. Long gone are the days when Amerindians landed their canoes here! From its beginnings as a natural harbour where boats landed right on the shore, the area became the port for Canada's metropolis and later a major international port. Today it is an historic port, offering Montrealers direct access to the St. Lawrence River and to St. Helen's Island and Notre-Dame Island—and whose landscape is the product of the cumulative layering and overlapping of port structures from the two major periods of development (the beginning of the nineteenth century and the beginning of the twentieth century) and the restoration done since.

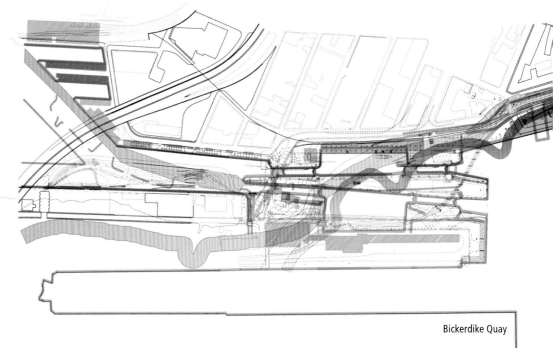

Bickerdike Quay

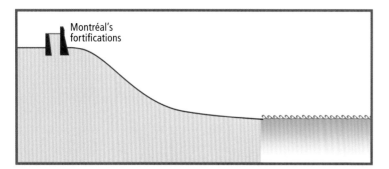

Montréal's fortifications

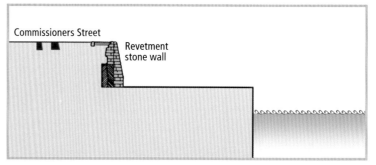

Commissioners Street

Revetment stone wall

1762

Around 1888

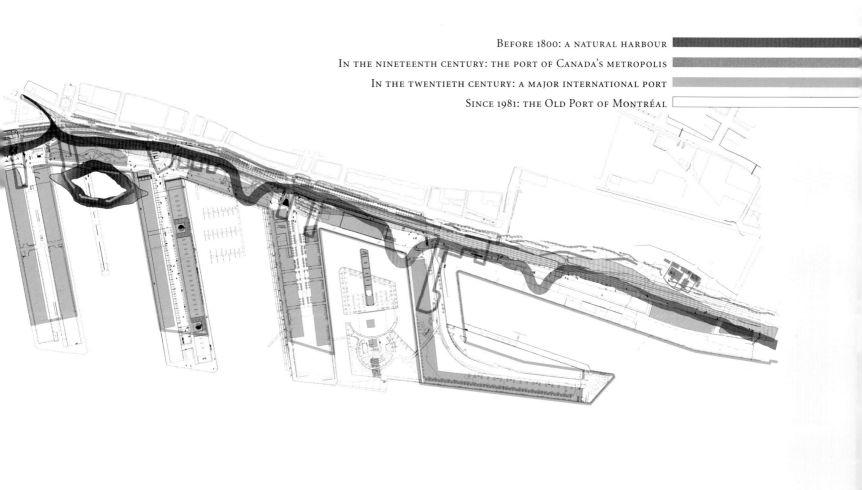

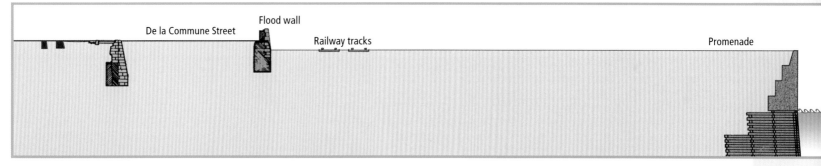

De la Commune Street

Flood wall

Railway tracks

Promenade

1930

2006

Since prehistoric times: a natural place to stop

The Montréal archipelago is a tremendous strategic asset, located as it is at the heart of waterways flowing into the Atlantic as well as leading into the centre of the continent. Thanks to its geographic location, the site was well suited for trade, although natural obstacles blocked the route for those wanting to sail up the St. Lawrence River. In 1535, French explorer Jacques Cartier, in order to reach Montréal, had to leave his galleon in Lake St. Pierre—in shallow waters—and continue on in a smaller craft. Beyond the harbour of Montréal, the turbulent Lachine Rapids kept him from continuing westward. However, it was precisely because of the necessity to stop here that the harbour of Montréal would, right from the beginning, play such a key role in the economic and social development of Canada.

Well before the first French explorers arrived, native peoples knew this was a point beyond which travel was difficult. Four millennia ago, nomadic groups stopped here, sometimes staying for short periods. From approximately the year 1000 onward, people stayed for longer and longer periods, until finally they settled permanently. Cartier noted this when he visited the Iroquois village of Hochelaga, near Mount Royal.

Nearly 70 years later, near the "Grand Sault St. Louis" rapids, Samuel de Champlain was to meet some natives who knew about a portage trail that bypassed the churning waters, where one of his fellow explorers met his death.

Evidence of prehistoric settlements is found in a number of archaeological sites in Montréal, and especially in Old Montréal. Traces of native encampments can be seen in the crypt of the Notre-Dame-de-Bon-Secours Chapel. However, most of these sites are found in the area near Pointe-à-Callière (Place Royale is one example), in the spot where a little river, later named the St. Pierre, flowed into the St. Lawrence. (This small waterway, which flowed under what is now Place d'You-ville, was channelled underground at the beginning of the nineteenth century. A section of its main conduit is visible at Pointe-à-Cal-lière, the Montréal Museum of Archaeology and History.) The existence of so many sites in one area indicates that this was a particularly accessible landing place.

When Champlain arrived in Montréal for the first time, in 1603, he dropped anchor near a small island facing the headland at the mouth of the little river; from that point on, the water was not deep enough for his boat to pass through.

In 1642, that same headland, with its natural advantages, saw the arrival of Paul Chomedey de Maisonneuve, Jeanne Mance and their companions, who had come from France to build a permanent settlement and spread the gospel to the native population. They founded Montréal at the junction of the little river and the St. Lawrence by building Fort Ville-Marie.

A harbour unchanged over time

Around 1815 (published in English in 1832), Joseph Bouchette (1776-1841), a surveyor-general for Lower Canada, described Montréal's harbour, at a time when the site still looked the same as when first seen by Cartier, Champlain and Maisonneuve.

The harbour of Montréal is not very large, but always secure for shipping during the time the navigation of the river is open. Vessels drawing fifteen feet water can lie close to the shore, near the Market-gate, to receive or discharge their cargoes: the general depth of water is from three to four and a half fathoms [1 fathom = 1.6 metres]*, with very good anchorage every where between the Market-gate Island and the shore: in the spring this island is nearly submerged by the rising of the river: but still it is always useful in protecting ships anchored within it from the violent currents of that period and at other times serves as a convenient spot for repairing boats, water-casks, and performing other indispensable works.*

IN 1642, MAISONNEUVE AND HIS COMPANIONS SETTLED ON THE HEADLAND AT THE MOUTH OF THE LITTLE ST. PIERRE RIVER, A SPOT WHICH WOULD LATER BE KNOWN AS THE "POINTE À CALLIÈRE". THIS PRINT, BY DONALD KENNETH ANDERSON AND ENTITLED *THE FOUNDING OF MONTRÉAL*, WAS DONE IN 1967 FOR CANADA'S CENTENNIAL.

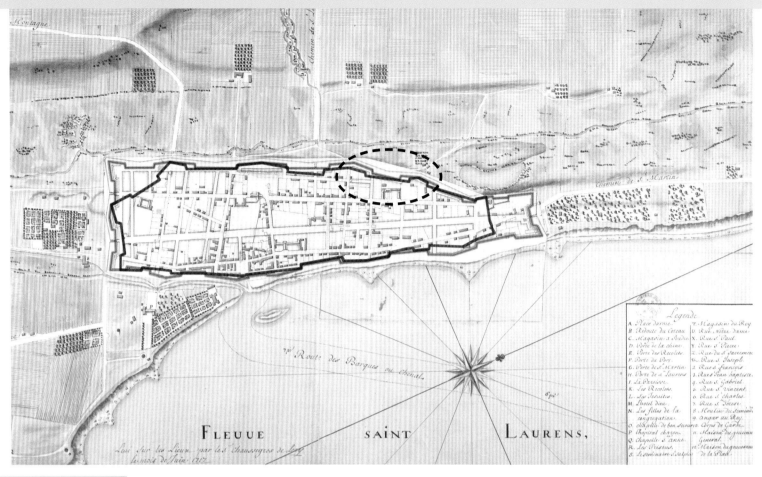

▬▬▬▬▬▬ WOODEN STOCKADE

▬▬▬▬▬▬ NEW FORTIFICATION WALL IN CUT STONE

– – – – – – PRESERVED SECTION IN CHAMPS DE MARS PARK

By the time several decades had passed, Fort Ville-Marie could no longer house the inhabitants of Montréal, especially as flooding was a recurring problem on the headland. As a result, the young colony began to expand along Coteau Saint-Louis, located on the other side of the Little St. Pierre River. Soon, Montréal was surrounded by a wooden palisade (1687-1717), which was in turn replaced by a higher masonry wall (1717-1817).

The economy of the small fortified city depended entirely on the fur trade. Pelts arriving from the west—from "up river", referring to the Great Lakes region—were unloaded at Lachine at the head of the rapids and transported to Montréal overland. Then they were loaded onto boats at the "little market island", the same small island near which Champlain had anchored his ship and which faced the first marketplace (today Place Royale). From there they were shipped to Quebec City where they were transferred onto ships sailing for Europe. At that time, only the deepwater port of Quebec City, with its stone quays, could harbour transatlantic ships. Only boats with less than three metres draught could travel up the St. Lawrence to Montréal.

Even unloading was more complicated in Montréal. Since the boats could not sail right to the shore, goods had to be transferred into canoes or unloaded onto horse-drawn carts driven right into the water to where the boat was moored!

As an embankment several metres high ran along the Montréal waterfront, ramps down to the water were built outside the city's main gates (from west to east, Market Gate, Castle Gate and Barracks Gate) to make it easier for people and carts to go up and down. The area around Callière's Point was the easiest to reach: it was outside the fortifications and the bank was not as high or as steep as elsewhere. From the end of the eighteenth century onward, wooden quays were built along the Point—some of which are mentioned on maps.

During this period, the city grew to a point where there was no room left inside the fortification wall. In 1801, in an attempt to make the city more attractive and resolve congestion, the "Act to Demolish the Old Walls and Fortifications Surrounding the City of Montréal" was adopted. It took fifteen years, from 1802 to 1817, to completely tear down the walls. Those on the south slope (the harbour front) were the first to go, followed by those on the north side.

This view of the harbour painted in 1800 by Richard Dillon shows the partially demolished fortifications and the city opening directly onto the river. Boats were anchored in the harbour and quays were virtually nonexistent. The banks of the river were accessed by cart. Timber was brought ashore in the form of large rafts known as "cages".

Only a few traces of the stone fortification walls have survived. A large section can be seen in Champs de Mars Park, behind Montréal's City Hall. Nearly 250 metres of the levelled remains of the scarp (inside wall) and the counterscarp (outside wall), with a ditch in between, can be seen.

1 Scarp

2 Ditch

3 Counterscarp

4 Glacis

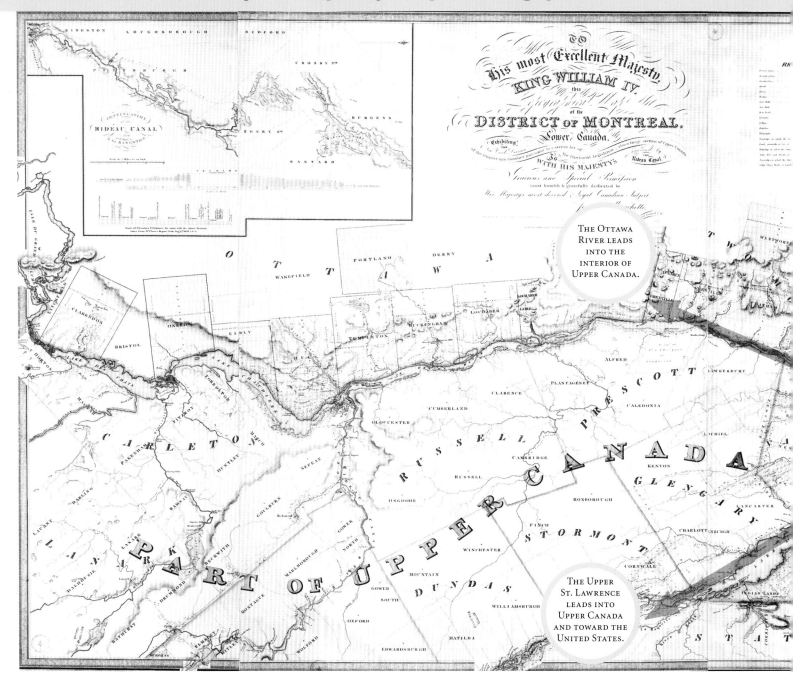

By the nineteenth century, Montréal had grown into a very lively city, with a largely British merchant elite. Soon the city would become Canada's metropolis and one of the major urban centres of North America.

The spectacular growth in population seen over the century—from 9,000 inhabitants in 1800 to nearly 280,000 in 1901!—was not only due, as in previous years, to the high birth rate of French-Canadian families. A massive flow of migrants into the city was also a contributing factor. In the first half of the nineteenth century, immigration was mainly from the British Isles, with a significant Irish component. Later, many francophones came: the countryside was overflowing and families moved by the thousands to New England . . . and into Quebec's large cities.

A sizable majority of the million immigrants who came to Canada between 1815 and 1850 chose to settle the fertile lands around the Great Lakes, which put Montréal right at the hub of back-and-forth river traffic. Many at the time harshly criticized the port's muddy banks. New infrastructure was needed, especially as the economy became more diversified.

In 1825, the opening of the Lachine Canal meant that boats could finally bypass the rapids (something merchants had been trying to promote for almost two hundred years). Gone was the difficult overland transfer of goods to Lachine. Very quickly, shipping traffic increased. It became absolutely necessary to develop a port worthy of the name. Just as in the past Champlain had been faced with

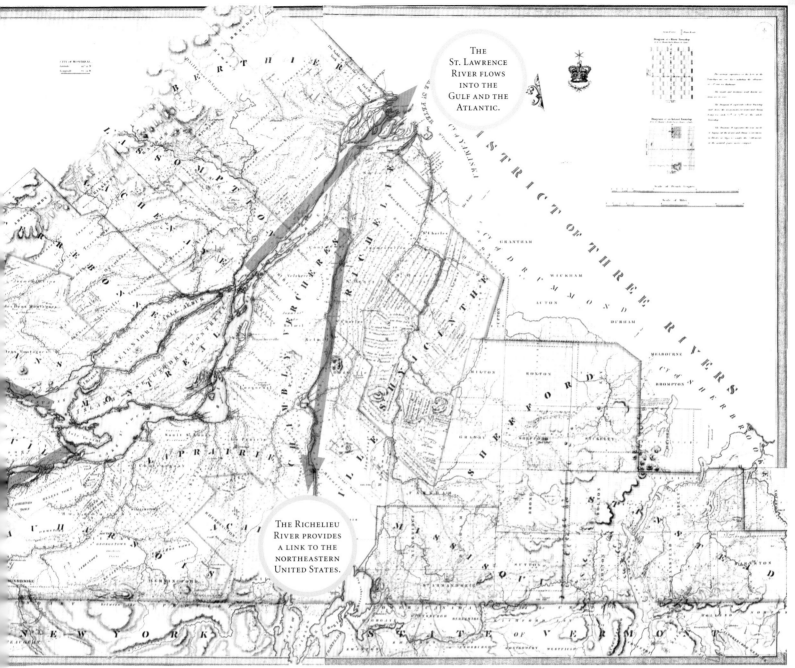

The
St. Lawrence
River flows
into the
Gulf and the
Atlantic.

The Richelieu
River provides
a link to the
northeastern
United States.

the need to "break bulk" (transfer goods from one means of transport to another), when merchant ships arrived from the east with cargo bound for the west, this cargo had to be transferred to boats that could fit into the Canal. This meant they had to stop in Montréal and . . . pay!

The Canal's presence had major economic repercussions, one being an increased workforce, since workers were needed to meet the boats, unload them, load the cargo, direct the passengers, and carry their suitcases. But in

order to reap the full benefits of this windfall, quays and sheds were needed . . . In 1830, the Montréal Harbour Commission was created, with a mandate to improve and expand the harbour.

The first three commissioners were Georges Moffat, Jules Quesnel and Captain Robert S. Piper, who drew up the redevelopment plans. These plans were carried out after being reviewed by engineer Peter Fleming.

At long last, the "Port of Montréal" had become a reality.

The Montréal archipelago (shown here in 1831) sits at a crossroads of waterways leading to the interior of Canada and the United States, and flowing into the Atlantic. A perfect location for trade, commerce and the accompanying movement of peoples.

MONTRÉAL AS SEEN FROM MOUNT ROYAL, AROUND 1860
THE CITY WAS GROWING AND INDUSTRIALIZING (NOTICE THE SMOKE EMERGING FROM THE FACTORY CHIMNEYS) AND REQUIRED MORE INFRASTRUCTURE. ALREADY, THE LACHINE CANAL PROVIDED NEARBY BUSINESSES WITH WATER FOR OPERATING TURBINES AND MACHINES, SUPPLYING STEAM ENGINES OR PARTICIPATING IN MANUFACTURING PROCESSES. DEVELOPING THE PORT ALSO BOOSTED THE NEW ECONOMY, AS DID THE NEWLY INAUGURATED VICTORIA BRIDGE (ABOVE RIGHT). THANKS TO THIS LINK THE RAIL NETWORK COULD NOW REACH ACROSS THE ST. LAWRENCE. THIS MAGNIFICENT ANONYMOUS ILLUSTRATION ALSO SHOWS NOTRE-DAME BASILICA, BONSECOURS MARKET AND ST. HELEN'S ISLAND AS THEY WERE AT THE TIME.

A harbourfront that could be seen from a distance

Let's step briefly back in time, not to the era of the Harbour Commissioners but to that of the men whose role it was to tear down the fortifications and change the layout of a number of streets. In the first phase of their "Commissioners Plan", they laid out a street along the waterfront, Commissioners Street (today De la Commune Street and Place d'Youville). From the 1820s on, buildings began to go up on the north side of the street. Some of these were new buildings. Others were extensions of house-stores whose business entrances opened onto St. Paul Street—or, in some cases, a new building attached to one of these joint residential and commercial buildings (in a few places the combination can still be seen). In other instances, a building on Commissioners Street would be built in front of another on St. Paul Street and they would share the courtyard in between. These first buildings were gradually replaced by multi-storied stone warehouse-stores, creating the long slightly winding frontage that makes up the remarkable waterfront we know today—a rarity in North America.

After 1831, another structure was built on the harbourfront: a long stone wall, with a series of access ramps connecting the street and the riverbank, like the ones in Paris on the quays of the Seine. It is this wall that authors of the day and visitors of the period referred to when they spoke of the "stone quay of Montréal"—the term "quay" meaning here a causeway along the water's edge. Above were the wooden landing facilities.

The stone wall was designed to protect Montrealers (with greater or lesser success) from the accumulation of winter ice and spring floods. But its real function was to support the natural embankment. Commissioners Street had to be wide and stable because of the heavy traffic: it was *the* street used by all travellers and goods transiting through the port, and a major commercial street, with its warehouse-stores, inns, hotels—even more so after the opening of Bonsecours Market (1847), which increased traffic considerably.

In this part of the city, as might be imagined, business activity revolved around the import-export trade. At the beginning, only a few warehouses had the right to bring in goods duty free, such as the Logan store (under 1 McGill Street). Shortly after Montréal was made a customs port (1832), the first customs house was built in Place Royale (between 1836 and 1838). Today the "Old Custom House" is part of Pointe-à-Callière.

IN THE NINETEENTH CENTURY, PLATT HOUSE, WHICH CAN STILL BE SEEN AT THE CORNER OF DE LA COMMUNE STREET AND ST. LAWRENCE BOULEVARD, WAS A WAREHOUSE-STORE. IT HAD A GABLE WITH A BLOCK AND TACKLE FOR HOISTING GOODS NEWLY ARRIVED IN THE PORT UP TO THE STORAGE FLOORS. LIKE OTHERS ON THE WATERFRONT, THE BUILDING OPENED ONTO ST. PAUL STREET—THE STOREFRONT ENCOURAGED CLIENTS TO GO IN AND BUY THE LATEST ITEMS.

Around 1875

ROYAL INSURANCE COMPANY

ACCESS RAMP

STONE WALL

WHEN THE QUAYS WERE RAISED AT THE BEGINNING OF THE TWENTIETH CENTURY, THE STONE WALL AND THE FIRST QUAYS WERE BURIED UNDER SEVERAL METRES OF FILL. THEIR REMAINS STILL LIE UNDER DE LA COMMUNE STREET AND THE OLD PORT RAILWAY LINES.

Rediscover a unique street

With a few exceptions, most of the buildings on De la Commune Street date from the nineteenth century. The oldest were built between 1820 and 1830. Among these are the Elizabeth Mittleberger Platt Warehouse, the Robert Unwin Harwood Building, the Pierre Beaudry Warehouse and the Bouthillier Warehouses. The latter, often incorrectly referred to as the Youville Stables, were built to store potash, one of the most important commodities exported to Great Britain at the beginning of the nineteenth century, and later used as offices and warehouses until they were restored in 1967.

Why not test your skill at locating all of these buildings as you stroll from west to east along the street?

Name	Adress	Construction Date
Commissioners Building	357 De la Commune Street West	1874-1878
Edmonstone, Allan & Co. Building	333 De la Commune Street West	1858-1859
Edmonstone, Allan & Co. Warehouse	366-368 Marguerite d'Youville Street	1867
Grey Nuns Stores II	329 De la Commune Street West	1873
John Try Warehouse VI	321-323 De la Commune Street West	1854-1855
John Try Warehouse V	315 De la Commune Street West	1854-1855
John Try Warehouse III	305-307 De la Commune Street West	1846
John Try Warehouse II	299 De la Commune Street West	c. 1831
John Try Warehouse I	295 De la Commune Street West	c. 1831
Masson Warehouse-Store	281-283 De la Commune Street West	1881
Bouthillier Warehouses	290-310 Place D'Youville	c. 1826-1828
Robert Gillespie Warehouse III	221 De la Commune Street West	1841-1842
Robert Gillespie Warehouse II	215-217 De la Commune Street West	1841-1842
Robert Gillespie Warehouse I	211 De la Commune Street West	1841-1842
Pierre Beaudry Warehouse	201-207 De la Commune Street West	1828
Harbour Commission Building	360 Place Royale	1853
Custom House (now the Old Custom House)	151 De la Commune Street West	1836-1838
Boyer's Block	133 De la Commune Street West	1857
Unnamed	121-123 De la Commune Street West	1853
Unnamed	109-119 De la Commune Street West	c. 1850
Jean Louis Beaudry Building	101-105 De la Commune Street West	1866
Greenshields Warehouse, Hodgson, Racine Ltd.	65-71 De la Commune Street West	1963
Charles Lamontagne Warehouse	61-63 De la Commune Street West	1830
Racine Warehouse-Store	57 De la Commune Street West	1886-1887
Esprit Généreux Warehouse-Store	47-55 De la Commune Street West	1886
Alfred Larocque Building	15 De la Commune Street West	1869
Robert Unwin Harwood Building	7-9 De la Commune Street West	1824-1825
Elizabeth Mittleberger Platt Warehouse	3 De la Commune Street West	1822-1823
Marie-Hélène Jodoin Warehouse-Store	3-5 De la Commune Street East	1872-1873
Unnamed	20-22 St. Paul Street East, also fronting on De la Commune	1846
Louis Archambeault Warehouse-Store	27 De la Commune Street East	1882-1883
Jean Leclaire Warehouse-Store	29 De la Commune Street East	1870
Narcisse Desmarteau Warehouse-Store	37 De la Commune Street East	1854
Victor Hudon Warehouse-Store I	84 St. Paul Street East, also fronting on De la Commune	c. 1855
Victor Hudon Warehouse-Store II	85-89 De la Commune Street East	c. 1855
Hector Lamontagne Warehouse-Store	97-101 De la Commune Street East	1882-1883
Amable Prévost Warehouse-Store I	103 De la Commune Street East	1864
Amable Prévost Warehouse-Store II	100 St. Paul Street East, also fronting on De la Commune	1864
Simon Valois Warehouse-Store	104 St. Paul Street East, also fronting on De la Commune	1858
Unnamed	110 St. Paul Street East, also fronting on De la Commune	1979
Alexandre Roy Warehouse-Store	115 De la Commune Street East	c. 1860
John Pratt Warehouse-Store	119-125 De la Commune Street East	1874-1875
Ricard Warehouse-Store	127-129 De la Commune Street East	1877-1878
Joseph-Auguste Laviolette Warehouse-Store	133 De la Commune Street East	1893
Victor Hudon Warehouse-Store	143 De la Commune Street East	1861
Unnamed (Canada Steamship Lines)	145 De la Commune Street East	1945
Unnamed	154 St. Paul Street East, also fronting on De la Commune	c. 1860
Thomas Wilson Warehouse-Store	158 St. Paul Street East, also fronting on De la Commune	1861
Thomas Tiffin Warehouse-Store	257 De la Commune Street East	1857
Unnamed	263-265 De la Commune Street East	1977
J. Roy Building	269 De la Commune Street East	c. 1860
Unnamed	277 De la Commune Street East	1845-1848
Bonsecours Market	305-395 De la Commune Street East	1844-1847
Notre-Dame-de-Bon-Secours Chapel	413 De la Commune Street East	1771-1773
Notre-Dame-de-Bon-Secours School	417 De la Commune Street East	1893
Bonneau Shelter	427 De la Commune Street East	1904?, 1998
Lymburner Building II	444 St. Paul Street East, also fronting on De la Commune	1904
Lymburner Building I	460 St. Paul Street East	1916
Unnamed	350-354 Berri Street (at de la Friponne Street)	1905

1860-1870

1873-1874

April 3, 1891

A long battle against ice and water

For a long time, the lowest lying land in Montréal was subject to flooding, which could happen in winter as well as in spring. There were many possible reasons (better understood today) and they could be different every time: an intense cold spell that would trigger the formation of *frazil*, a mixture of ice and water that slowed down the flow and sometimes blocked a waterway to the point where the ice rose and water flooded the banks; rapid snow melt; sudden ice jams; or a convergence of several of these factors.

On their very first Christmas in Montréal, December 25, 1642, the Sieur de Maisonneuve and his companions watched as the waters of the St. Lawrence rose and rose higher still . . . to the point where Fort Ville-Marie was threatened. Luckily, the waters subsided before causing any significant damage. To thank God for having protected them, the French settlers went in a procession to plant a cross at the top of Mount Royal, an event that the Saint John the Baptist Society commemorated in 1924 when it erected the cross that stands there today.

In the nineteenth century, the port authorities and the citizens of Montréal were still regularly faced with problems caused by water and ice pushing violently against the quays and banks. A great deal of effort was put into trying to control these elements: a stone wall, a wooden landing stage . . . but there were years when nothing worked.

In 1886, a particularly strong flood revived the idea of a barrier, which had been called for by merchants for decades. "Mackay Pier", whose construction began in 1891, kept on being improved until 1967, when it became what it is today: the Cité du Havre. Along with the flood wall (whose construction began in 1899 as a replacement for the former stone wall, rising 56 centimetres above the highest level ever reached by the flood waters), this long ice-deflecting pier has played a major role in permanently protecting the lower town from flooding. That said, the effects of rising waters are still felt around the island, as news bulletins regularly remind us.

1870-1880

THE STONE WALL, WITH A
BLOCKADE . . . A VIEW THAT
UNDERLINES THE EXTENT
OF THE FACILITIES BUILT TO
WARD OFF WATER AND ICE.

1869

Around 1886

THE WALL OF THE ALLAN
BUILDING, NOW THE HEAD
OFFICE OF THE OLD PORT OF
MONTRÉAL CORPORATION,
AT 333, DE LA COMMUNE
STREET WEST, BEARS A MARK
SHOWING HOW HIGH THE
WATERS ROSE DURING THE
GREAT FLOOD OF 1886.

1886

ON THE RIGHT
FROM TOP TO BOTTOM

FLOODING IN ST. PAUL
STREET, AS FAR UP
AS ST. PIERRE STREET.

VIEW TOWARDS THE
RIVER FROM . . . PLACE
JACQUES-CARTIER.

VICTORIA SQUARE
FLOODED.

IN FRONT OF THE
CUSTOM HOUSE,
ON THE ST. PAUL
STREET SIDE.

December 16, 1871

February 4, 1882

Around 1870

Around 1886

A PORT THAT FROZE
IN THE WINTER AND
FLOODS THAT ENGULFED
THE QUAYS, SHEDS
AND STREETS IN THE
SPRING . . . IN THE
NINETEENTH CENTURY,
SUDDEN CLIMATIC
EVENTS REGULARLY
UPSET MONTREALERS'
DAILY ROUTINE.

**By carriage?
By canoe more likely!**
During the great flood of 1886, the waters reached the spot where the former Bonaventure Station stood. This is now the site of the Montréal Planetarium, at the corner of Peel and St. James streets.

1865-1875

2006

Then and now

THE PHOTOGRAPH ON THE
LEFT GIVES THE IMPRESSION
THAT RIVER ICE HAS REACHED
COMMISSIONERS STREET.
IN FACT, THE PHOTOGRAPHER
TOOK THE PICTURE FROM THE
QUAYS. ALTHOUGH THE ROYAL
INSURANCE BUILDING WAS
TORN DOWN IN 1947, THE
FOOTPRINT OF ITS DISTINCTIVE
TRIANGULAR SHAPE LIVES ON
IN THE OUTLINE OF
POINTE-à-CALLIÈRE, THE
MONTRÉAL MUSEUM OF
ARCHAEOLOGY AND HISTORY.

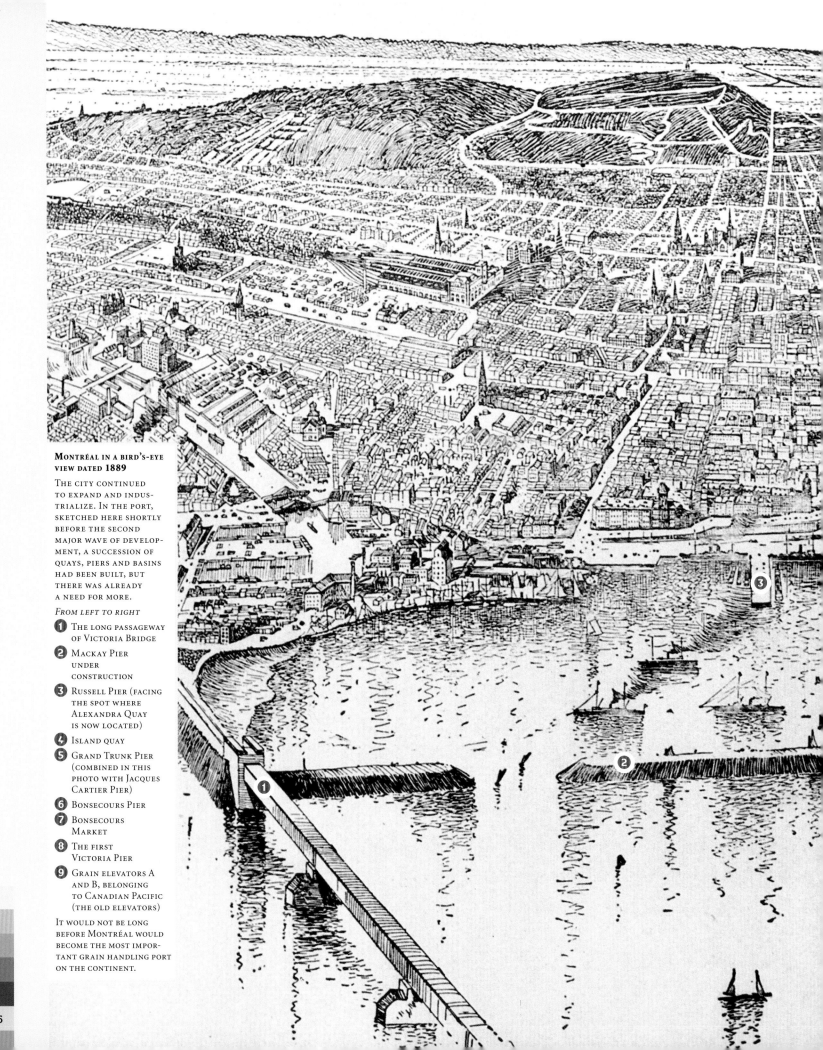

MONTRÉAL IN A BIRD'S-EYE VIEW DATED 1889

The city continued to expand and industrialize. In the port, sketched here shortly before the second major wave of development, a succession of quays, piers and basins had been built, but there was already a need for more.

From left to right

1. The long passageway of Victoria Bridge
2. Mackay Pier under construction
3. Russell Pier (facing the spot where Alexandra Quay is now located)
4. Island quay
5. Grand Trunk Pier (combined in this photo with Jacques Cartier Pier)
6. Bonsecours Pier
7. Bonsecours Market
8. The first Victoria Pier
9. Grain elevators A and B, belonging to Canadian Pacific (the old elevators)

It would not be long before Montréal would become the most important grain handling port on the continent.

More quays and piers were added and later modified

From 1830 on, the Harbour Commissioners had many wooden quays and piers built below the stone wall and ramps. (It is important here to explain how these two terms are used in this book. A quay, strictly speaking, is a structure that runs along a shore, while a pier projects far out into the water—either parallel or perpendicular to the current. That said, we now commonly refer to what are actually piers as Alexandra Quay, King Edward Quay, Jacques Cartier Quay and Clock Tower Quay.)

The small island near which Samuel de Champlain anchored his ship in 1603, facing the mouth of the Little St. Pierre River, was the first to have a wooden quay built: it was covered with boards and linked to the main bank by a pier. The result was a calm basin for boats.

Other infrastructure was built around the port for specific purposes.

Upstream, the first quays along Callière's Point were gradually replaced by a series of quays, piers and basins (Russell, Wellington, Nelson . . .). These facilities were mainly used for transferring passengers and goods heading west, via the Lachine Canal.

Downstream, other piers were built. Facing the new market (today Place Jacques Cartier), Grand Trunk Pier and Jacques Cartier Pier accommodated ferries and passenger boats heading eastward. In front of Bonsecours Market, a quay was built for the farmers and merchants of the region. Bonsecours Pier was added to it in 1859. Further along still, Victoria Pier (which would be replaced by a new pier of the same name and then renamed Clock Tower Quay in 1992) and a military quay completed the series.

Starting in 1899, all the facilities dating from the nineteenth century were abandoned and replaced, the better to cater to the needs of transatlantic ships, which required a deeper draught and rose to an equally great height above the water, and to meet the new demands of a growing grain economy. Thus appeared the quays and piers that still characterize the Old Port, from Alexandra Quay to Clock Tower Quay, and including Conveyor Quay, the last to be constructed in 1956-1957.

1859

ISLAND QUAY, THE FIRST "OFFICIAL" QUAY IN THE PORT OF MONTRÉAL. THE SMALL ISLAND WAS ATTACHED TO THE SHORE IN 1832. IT WAS LOCATED ON THE SITE OF THE CURRENT CONVEYOR QUAY.

1865

FERRIES BELONGING TO THE RICHELIEU COMPANY, ONE OF THE PREDECESSORS OF CANADA STEAMSHIP LINES (TODAY PART OF CSL GROUP INC.), WERE MOORED AROUND GRAND TRUNK PIER AND JACQUES CARTIER PIER.

1884

Bonsecours Pier and Basin welcomed merchants who came to sell their products in the market of the same name, seen just opposite.

1885

The port of Montréal, photographed from Canadian Pacific Elevator A (no longer standing). The stone wall separating Commissioners Street from the wooden quays below is clearly visible.

Victoria Pier and its basin, before it was replaced by a new Victoria Pier (now Clock Tower Quay).

1910

THE PORT OF MONTRÉAL, SHOWN HERE IN 1887
IN THE NINETEENTH CENTURY, IMPORTED PRODUCTS ARRIVED IN BULK: WINES AND SPIRITS—ESPECIALLY RUM—, SALT, TEA, COFFEE, SUGAR, COAL AND OTHER GOODS, AS WELL AS MANUFACTURED PRODUCTS, HARDWARE, CLOTHING AND TEXTILES, ETC. EXPORTS CONSISTED MAINLY OF POTASH, PEARL ASH (A DERIVATIVE OF POTASH), AND WHEAT, FLOUR AND WOOD, RATHER THAN THE FURS OF THE PREVIOUS CENTURY.

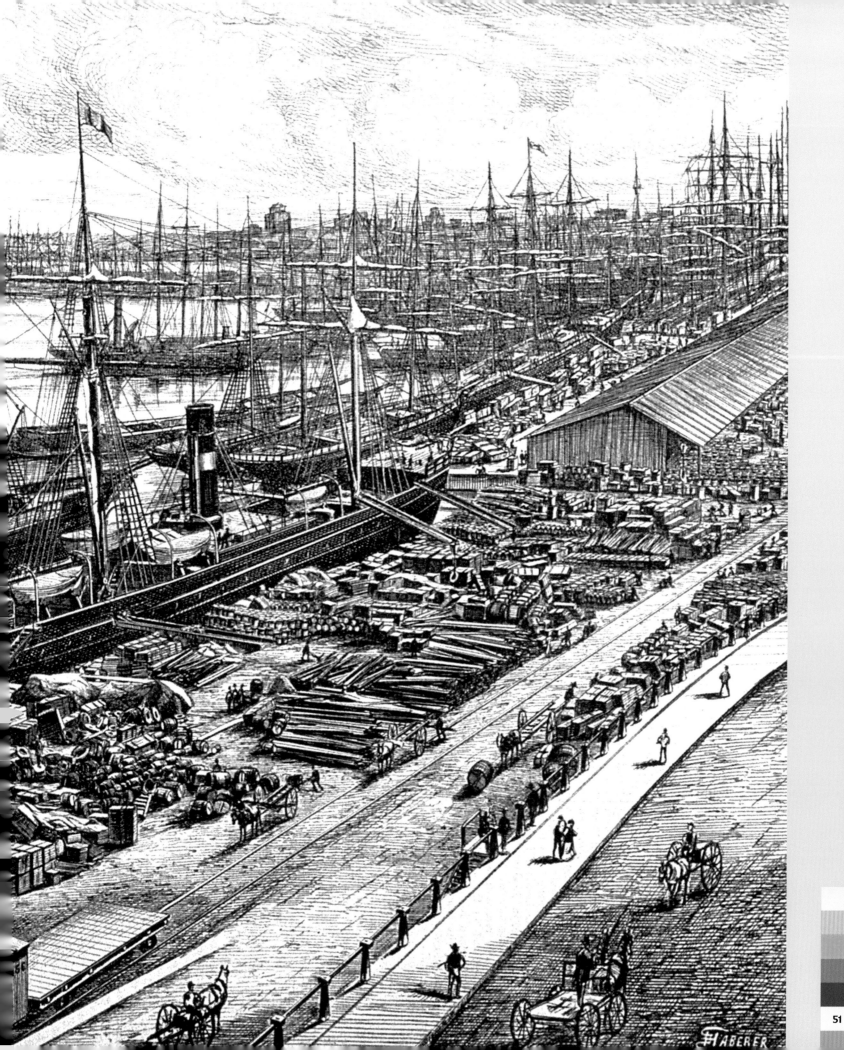

Quay construction techniques continued to improve

The materials and techniques used in building the port's quays and piers changed markedly over the decades.

From 1846 on, the first wooden quays built on pine and oak piles began to be replaced by structures built on cribs, horizontal pieces of wood piled up to the desired height and filled with earth and stones. This technique had certain advantages. When the upper portion of a pile deteriorated, the whole pile had to be replaced, whereas with a crib structure only the damaged portions above the water level had to be replaced.

When the quays were raised at the beginning of the twentieth century, cribwork was again used, but so was a new material, concrete. It was much more resistant than wood, which deteriorated rather quickly under the combined effect of landing shocks, the movement of water and fluctuations in temperature and humidity. However, wood immersed in water could last for hundreds of years. The authorities decided to reap the benefits of both materials: concrete for surfaces exposed to air and wood for those underwater.

The cribworks built around 1900 are so well preserved that they still exist below the water's surface under all of the quays of the Old Port. Under the quays on the promenade, when the water level is very low in July and August, they can still be glimpsed below the concrete wall. This is not the case with the long quays that project into the water. Although cribs still lie under the centre of these structures, the former piers have since been covered with concrete. They have been widened, strengthened and lengthened using a combination of cylindrical concrete piles, concrete walls and concrete cribs.

THE CRIBWORK OF A MODERN QUAY, BEFORE AND AFTER (BELOW) BEING STRENGTHENED WITH CONCRETE PILES.

Clever and sturdy construction methods

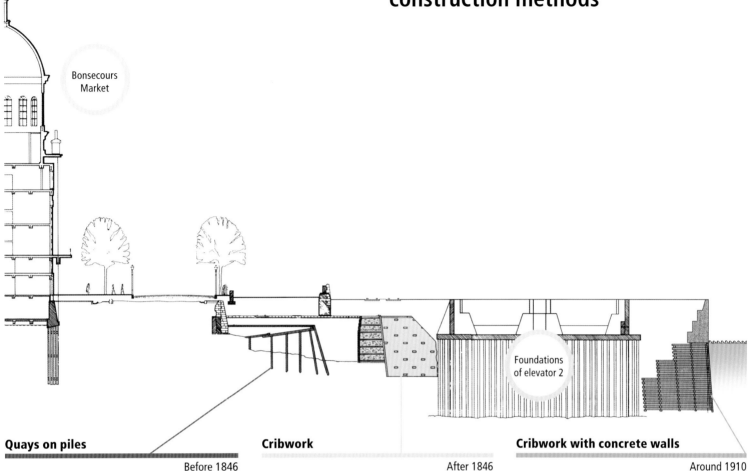

Bonsecours Market

Foundations of elevator 2

Quays on piles

Before 1846

To construct the Island Quay in 1830, as well as others later built along the embankment, the Montréal Harbour Commission used the following technique. Squared pine piles, each side of which measured 30 to 35 centimetres, were first driven two metres deep into the riverbed and assembled using oak fasteners and metal braces. Then, earth and rocks—often brought in from the Lachine Canal excavation—were packed in behind. Lastly, the whole area was covered with crushed stones (macadam). These quays were so solid that some of them lasted until the turn of the twentieth century, even though at the time engineers had given them a life expectancy of just 20 years. In the end, they were buried because the redevelopment of the port required it.

Cribwork

After 1846

A new construction technique began to be used: *cribwork*. Hewn pieces of wood were arranged in squares, piled one on top of the other and assembled using metal braces. The inside of the square was then filled in with earth and stones. This technique was especially useful for building piers that would project far out into the water, because nature herself could be harnessed to help: when ice filled the port, the cribs could be dragged to the desired locations and when the ice melted they would simply settle into place.

Cribwork with concrete walls

Around 1910

At the turn of the twentieth century, the cribwork technique was still being used for quays and piers. Since boats required deeper and deeper water, however, this technique was modified: cribs were placed on top of each other in a step-like arrangement, rather than vertically straight up, so that they could be piled higher and still be stable.

Over time, the submerged portion of the cribwork was replaced by an imposing concrete wall, as seen along the Old Port promenade and along Victoria Pier (Clock Tower Quay). Elsewhere, metal piles filled with concrete were used to widen the surface of the quays and strengthen the structure of the cribwork.

Shed 13 Shed 12 Shed 11

1908

The storage sheds: from temporary to permanent structures

In a port, goods are constantly being loaded and unloaded. In the nineteenth century, these operations took place right on the quays. The first sheds were used mainly by shipping companies, to receive passengers and house administration services. What's more, the buildings could only be used in summer: put up in the spring, they were taken down in the fall, before ice or flooding could carry them away.

At the beginning of the twentieth century, however, raising the quays made it possible to build permanent sheds, used to store goods for brief periods and to protect them from bad weather and theft before they were delivered or forwarded. Between 1904 and 1920, about twenty of these long buildings were built, after much discussion among their users—ship owners, shipping agents, railway companies, business people—and the Minister of Public Works. In the construction of these buildings, the Montréal Harbour Commissioners, after

having reviewed several sets of plans submitted by port engineer John Kennedy and visited the large American ports (including those of New York and Philadelphia), decided to combine several materials. The steel frame was covered with corrugated galvanized sheet iron and the main pillars were built on a concrete foundation, itself sitting on metal or wooden pillars.

In the 1980s, a number of the sheds were demolished. But others, in line with the 1990 redevelopment plan, have survived—in one form or another.

On Jacques Cartier Quay, these sheds are no longer standing. However, several features of the site remind us of what they looked like. On the former foundations, the architects of the Old Port have installed open modules showing how the sheds were once laid out and at the same time providing space for a variety of uses. As for the Jacques Cartier Pavilion, opened in 1992, its architecture also evokes

the layout of the old sheds, including the long walkway that formerly ran along the second floor of this type of building.

On King Edward Quay, the former sheds have been transformed into a space focussed on the present and the future, the Montréal Science Centre. Their steel framework was preserved and can actually be seen from inside the building.

On Alexandra Quay, for which the Montréal Port Authority and not the Old Port is responsible, the sheds still exist in their original layout. They have been modified just enough to suit their current uses: housing the Iberville Passenger Terminal, the Mariners' House and the operations of the Old Port.

Several other sheds, still in good condition, are used as parking lots. What should be done with these buildings in the long term is under discussion however.

Shed 16, on Clock Tower Quay, has the best preserved exterior.

1890

1908

1908, ON KING EDWARD PIER. THE LAST RIVET IN SHED 11 WAS HAMMERED IN, MARKING THE OFFICIAL OPENING OF THE FIRST PERMANENT SHEDS IN THE PORT OF MONTRÉAL.

SHED 16, AS IT APPEARS TODAY, TO THE EAST OF BONSECOURS BASIN. IT IS AWAITING RESTORATION.

LEFT
THE LONG SILHOUETTE OF JACQUES CARTIER PAVILION RECALLS THAT OF THE SHEDS IT REPLACED. NOTE, ON THE SECOND LEVEL, THE WALKWAY THAT WAS ALSO TYPICAL OF THE STORAGE SHEDS.

ABOVE
THE MODULES ON JACQUES CARTIER QUAY REMIND US SYMBOLICALLY OF THE CONFIGURATION OF THE FORMER SHEDS.

The former lives of the storage sheds of the Old Port

The sheds of the Old Port hold many memories . . . From the day they were built, many kinds of goods passed through the sheds: hay, boards, floor coverings, flour, sugar, cheese, apples, peas, wines and spirits, etc. Soon regulations were enacted. Since some goods transported in bulk were difficult to handle, the port announced that coal, for example, would henceforth have to be packed in bags. It became obvious that salt, salted hides and caustic substances were bad for the sheds' steel structure; soon, their storage was no longer allowed. In 1937, it was the Cunard Line's turn to complain. Grain dust continually blew out of the conveyor galleries and there was no way that Cunard would agree to pay for the cost of cleaning sheds 2 and 3, used for passenger traffic. The port therefore began to hire men to do the work.

Goods were transferred from railway cars to the sheds and then onto ships, partly using manpower, but also by means of equipment of greater or lesser sophistication—that was constantly being improved. From simple chutes to carts, elevators, transporters, cranes and marine legs, a whole range of infrastructure was developed, each adding a page to our shipping history.

In 1909, notably, the Montréal Harbour Commissioners had plans drawn up for freight elevators that, like those in Glasgow, could hold a vehicle pulled by two horses and weighing 5 tonnes. The term "team", used at the time for a team of two horses, thus became synonymous with load, whether in the new elevators or for goods hoisted by electric cranes—a semantic change that underlines the rapid developments in means of transportation and handling at the beginning of the twentieth century. The first freight elevators, brought from England, seem to have been the models for the ones the Harbour Commissioners ordered in 1913 from Dominion Bridge. The first freight elevator delivered by the company could hold two teams at once. It was installed in 1914 in the middle of Alexandra Pier. In 1925, when electric wiring was installed to run the trains, the freight elevators were moved right into the sheds.

1928

TWO *TEAMS* COULD FIT INTO A FREIGHT ELEVATOR.

At the beginning of the 1930s, the shipping companies that used the port were in the throes of the Great Depression. They therefore asked the authorities if they could use the sheds on a daily basis rather than sign an annual or seasonal lease, as had been the norm. That decision would come back to haunt them: when the economy got back on its feet in the middle of the decade and especially after the second World War, the companies were not allowed to reserve all of the sheds that they needed on an annual basis, despite many requests.

We should also note that during the two World Wars, the sheds were used entirely or in part by National Defence. Flour and other food products, hay and horses passed through the sheds while waiting to be put on board ship. During the 1939-1945 war, the Department used the sheds to store steel for factories run by the allies, munitions made in Canada and foodstuffs that were being sent to the war front. At the time, the waters of the St. Lawrence were virtually closed to merchant ships, and the shipping agents had little choice but to cancel their leases: moreover, several of their boats had been requisitioned by military authorities to transport men and goods.

A MASTERLY TRANSFORMATION
THE ARCHITECTS OF THE MONTRÉAL SCIENCE CENTRE NOT ONLY PRESERVED BUT ALSO HIGHLIGHTED THE STEEL FRAMES OF SOME OF THE SHEDS ON KING EDWARD QUAY—BUILT AT THE BEGINNING OF THE TWENTIETH CENTURY TO STORE GOODS IN TRANSIT. THE BUILDING THUS PRESERVES THE ORIGINAL VOLUMETRY. THE SECTIONS THAT HAVE NOT BEEN REDEVELOPED CURRENTLY PROVIDE PARKING FOR VISITORS.

TAKEN FROM A PIER, THIS
PHOTO SHOWS A SHED ON THE
LEFT. THE WALKWAY IS
CLEARLY VISIBLE, RUNNING
THE FULL LENGTH OF THE
BUILDING AND, ON THE ROOF,
THE OVERHEAD CONVEYOR
GALLERY CAN BE SEEN.
ATTACHED TO THE GALLERY
WERE TWO MOVABLE SPOUTS
THROUGH WHICH GRAIN WAS
POURED INTO THE HOLDS OF
SHIPS BERTHED ALONGSIDE.

DURING THE TWO WORLD
WARS, THE MINISTER
OF NATIONAL DEFENCE
REQUISITIONED THE SHEDS
IN THE PORT TO STORE ARMS
AND COMMODITIES DESTINED
FOR CANADIAN TROOPS. THIS
PHOTO WAS TAKEN IN 1914.

By boat but also by train

At the end of the nineteenth century, the port of Montréal became a true hub for shipping and railway networks. These networks came together and complemented each other in an especially remarkable way, whereas in the United States trains often competed with boats, and canals were filled in so that new railway lines could be laid overtop.

The first Canadian railway company, the Champlain and St. Lawrence Railway, was inaugurated in 1836, shortly after the Montréal Harbour Commission was created. From the port of Montréal, goods and passengers travelled by ferry to link up with the line connecting La Prairie and Saint-Jean d'Iberville (today Saint-Jean-sur-Richelieu) and from there they embarked for New York.

In 1851, the rail network expanded southward. Henceforth, it was possible to travel by train from Montréal to Boston. Then, in 1853, another line was added, this time linking Montréal to Portland (Maine). At that time, Montréal's Harbour Commissioners realized the importance of a rail link along which goods could be transported to the Atlantic seaboard during the winter, when ice prevented navigation on the St. Lawrence. Portland was chosen as Montréal's "winter port". However, it was still necessary to find a way for trains to cross the river.

The recently formed Grand Trunk Railway Company of Canada (which later became Canadian National Railways) won the bidding.

GTR bought the newly laid Montréal to Portland line and began to build the missing link: Victoria Bridge. In 1860, after an intense construction period, Victoria Bridge was inaugurated by the Prince of Wales amidst much pomp. It would be necessary to wait until 1871, however, for the first tracks to be laid on the quays of Montréal's port.

In 1881, another railway company was incorporated: the Canadian Pacific Railway Company, whose task it was to connect Montréal to a whole new Canadian province, British Columbia. The company built Dalhousie Station (on the corner of Berri and Notre-Dame streets) and on June 28, 1886, its first passenger train reached Port Moody after a comfortable seven-day trip. Not bad in an era when the stagecoach was still king of the West!

In 1910, more construction: as the quays were raised, so were the railway lines. And since the quays in the downstream section of the port remained at a lower level and the rail lines had to run on a horizontal plane, tunnels were built so that carts, vehicles and trucks using the main streets could pass under the railway tracks to get to the quays. Nowadays only the Berri Street tunnel, restored during redevelopment work in 1984, can still be used. The Bonneau Street tunnel has been filled in, as has a portion of the Beaudry Street tunnel, from which vehicles could enter the cold storage warehouse and whose north side can still be seen from the Papineau exit ramp on the Ville-Marie Autoroute.

When the Old Port of Montréal Corporation took over the old section of the port in the early 1980s, it had six of the eight remaining train tracks removed. There are thus only two remaining (with from one to three tracks, depending on the location) and they still connect the east and west sections of the port of Montréal. A new railway bridge was also built in the early 1990s in front of and above Lock 1 on the Lachine Canal—when the mouth of the canal was excavated, automobile and rail routes had to be redirected.

It should also be noted that three generations of trains have run through the port of Montréal. From 1871 onward, the trains were pulled by steam locomotives. Then, with improvements in electricity, the first electric locomotives, which were less polluting, came into use in 1923—powered by means of overhead lines similar to those used by tramways. The authorities were at first very proud of them, but the trains did not perform as well as expected: they were not powerful enough, at least according to Sir Alexander Gibb, who recommended, in 1935, a return to the old steam locomotives. Eventually, after 1951, these were replaced by others with diesel engines.

A surprising archaeological discovery

In 1990, during redevelopment work carried out by the Old Port at the entrance to the Lachine Canal, the author of this book made a surprising discovery with her team under the embankment along De la Commune Street: nine narrow-gauge railway tracks, narrower than those used by steam trains and all laid out perpendicular to the Canal! Even before locomotives came into use, from the 1820s onward merchants doing business along De la Commune and Wellington Streets had had these tracks laid so goods could be transported directly back and forth between the canal and their warehouses—in wagons pulled by men or horses. A few similar finds of this type have been recorded in the United States, but this is the only known example in Canada. The tracks now lie protected by the embankment under which they were buried.

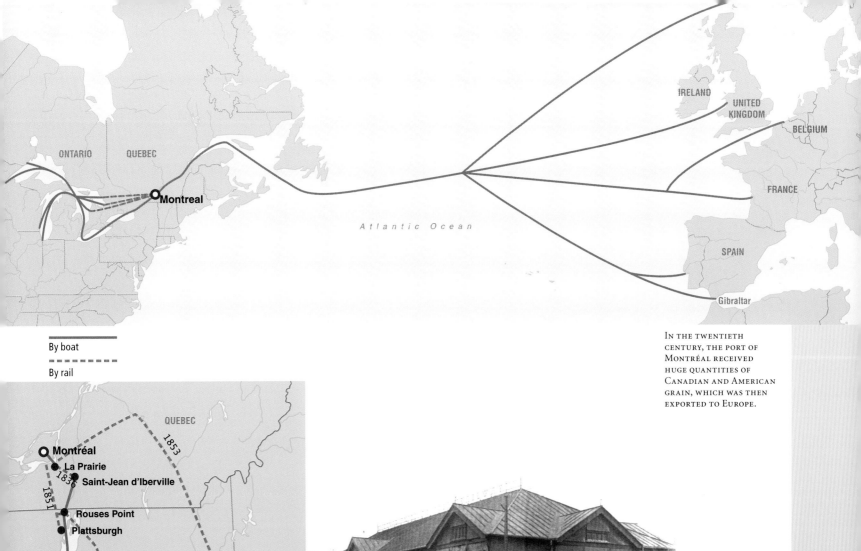

By boat

— — — — — —

By rail

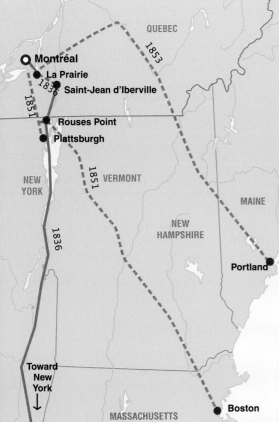

Montréal
La Prairie
1836
1851
Saint-Jean d'Iberville
1853
Rouses Point
Plattsburgh
QUEBEC
NEW YORK
1836
1851
VERMONT
NEW HAMPSHIRE
MAINE
Portland
Toward New York ↓
MASSACHUSETTS
Boston

THE GRADUAL EXPANSION OF THE RAILWAY NETWORK BETWEEN 1830 AND 1850
By 1860, Victoria Bridge enabled clients of the Grand Trunk Railway to travel or ship goods from Montréal to Portland or Boston and, by combining rail and boat transportation, all the way to New York.

IN THE TWENTIETH CENTURY, THE PORT OF MONTRÉAL RECEIVED HUGE QUANTITIES OF CANADIAN AND AMERICAN GRAIN, WHICH WAS THEN EXPORTED TO EUROPE.

DALHOUSIE STATION, BUILT IN 1883-84, WAS RESTORED IN 1986. TODAY IT IS HOME TO THE CIRQUE ÉLOIZE.

THE RAILWAY BRIDGE AT THE MOUTH OF THE LACHINE CANAL PROVIDED A LINK TO WINDMILL POINT AND BICKERDIKE QUAYS.

Victoria Bridge

When Victoria Bridge, built by the Grand Trunk Railway Company of Canada, was inaugurated in 1860, newspapers extolled it as the eighth wonder of the world. And with just cause, for the creative design and construction techniques that made it possible to build a bridge across the river were indeed ingenious. With its long metal passageway that had room for only one train at a time, this railway bridge evoked, albeit on a grander scale, the picturesque covered bridges seen in the countryside. In 1898, the tubular structure, lacking sufficient ventilation, was replaced by the current openwork structure. This made it possible to build two adjacent railway tracks with a toll lane on either side, one for vehicles (trams and cars) and one for pedestrians. Nowadays, the bridge is used only by trains and cars.

1873

The initial tubular structure of Victoria Bridge, built for trains only, was replaced in 1898 by a Howe type truss structure for mixed use: rail and road.

Around 1878

1906

In the first half of the twentieth century, the port of Montréal became the main North American grain port. In 1926, for example, it exported 135,000,000 bushels of grain (one bushel = 36.36 litres), compared with "only" 75,465,000 from New York!

Wheat from the Canadian and American west arrived either by boat, in vessels specially adapted for navigation on the St. Lawrence canal system, or by train. It was then loaded onto transatlantic ships and shipped mainly to England. Of course, in the winter the port was closed to shipping. But despite the slowdown in exports, the port continued to operate thanks to its very efficient infrastructure, as trains kept coming into the port, though there were very few of them. The elevators were used for storage rather than for the quick turnover of goods as in the summer.

From the 1960s onward, changing market conditions and new transshipping techniques would make the facilities of the old part of the port obsolete. Nonetheless, traces of what was once a hive of activity are still visible in the landscape of the Old Port.

FOR MANY YEARS, THE PORT AUTHORITIES USED THE INGENIOUS FLOATING ELEVATOR TO TRANSFER GRAIN FROM ONE BOAT TO ANOTHER. THIS WAS A TOWER ON PONTOONS, WHOSE MECHANISM WAS DRIVEN BY A STEAM ENGINE. ON ONE SIDE IT HAD A BUCKET CONVEYOR (A DEVICE INVENTED AT THE END OF THE EIGHTEENTH CENTURY BY MILLWRIGHT OLIVER EVANS AND LATER REFINED IN CHICAGO IN 1846 BY JOSEPH DART AND ROBERT DUNBAR) AND ON THE OTHER A TUBULAR FUNNEL KNOWN AS A SPOUT. THE FIRST FLOATING ELEVATOR APPEARED IN THE PORT OF MONTRÉAL IN 1857. BY THE END OF THE NINETEENTH CENTURY, THERE WERE SEVENTEEN. BY 1924, ONLY FIVE REMAINED. IN THE PHOTO ON THE RIGHT, WHERE TWO FLOATING ELEVATORS CAN BE SEEN, IT IS CLEAR THAT THEIR STRUCTURE HAS CHANGED, MAKING THEM MORE LIKE THE MARINE TOWERS ON SHORE.

1909

1920

An ingenious grain transshipping system

Designed by engineer John S. Metcalf, the grain transshipping system in the port of Montréal consisted of, for each grain elevator, at least one *marine tower* used to unload grain cargo from the ship and a series of moving belts or *conveyors* that carried the grain to the elevator—where it would await transfer to ocean-going vessels destined for Europe, or, more rarely, to a rail line.

To ensure that the grain was protected at all times from bad weather, the conveyors were installed in *galleries* running along the top of the sheds or (in the case of Conveyor Quay) through a tunnel. Some of the galleries had pouring spouts. When a spout was attached to one of the many chutes spaced along the gallery, grain could be poured right into the open holds of an outward bound ship.

The port had two large "units" for transshipping, in other words, two complete sets of infrastructure (quay-marine tower-conveyor-elevator). A grain carrier berthing in King Edward Basin would be unloaded by means of the two marine towers on Conveyor Quay.

As the towers were rail-mounted, they could be positioned so as to unload a large ship more quickly or to unload two ships at the same time. From there, the grain could be moved to nearby elevator 1, no longer in existence (the Eau-Canada garden now stands on the site). But a grain carrier docking instead in Jacques Cartier Basin (now Bonsecours Basin) would also have all the transshipping equipment required: it would be unloaded by the marine tower that stood at the time on pier 2. This tower, in contrast with the towers on Conveyor Quay, was not mobile. However, it had *two* marine legs or bucket conveyors, which meant it could just as easily empty the holds of a ship docked on the west side of the pier as those of one located on the east side. From there, the grain could be transferred to elevator 2 just a few steps away, between Bonsecours Basin and Commissioners Street, across from Bonsecours Market.

However, and therein lies the beauty of the system designed by Metcalf—*and the reason why the port of Montréal was so amazingly ef-*

ficient—, all the components of these two transhipping units were *interconnected* by conveyors, which even ran along the top of the storage sheds on Victoria Pier, further east. Grain transport was therefore not limited to the shortest boat-to-elevator route: grain from a boat unloaded by a marine tower could be moved to any elevator; the reverse was also true, as a boat docked at any quay could receive grain from any elevator—not necessarily the nearest. This meant that there was no time wasted in waiting and no space that was left unoccupied, or at least as little as possible! In addition, grain could be transferred directly from one boat to another using "floating elevators".

Today, the grain handling facilities that were so innovative and efficient at the beginning of the twentieth century are no longer as necessary: many ships carrying bulk cargo are now equipped with a self-unloading system that works both for transferring cargo from one ship to another and for unloading onto the quays.

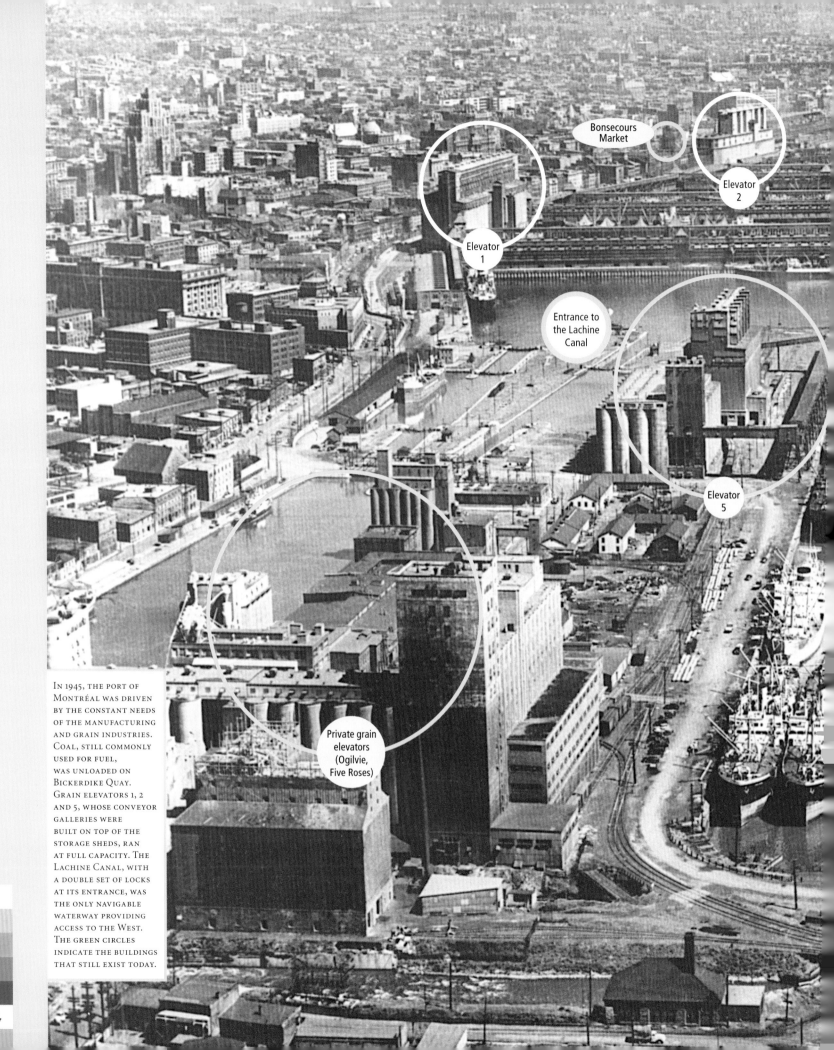

Bonsecours
Market

Elevator
2

Elevator
1

Entrance to
the Lachine
Canal

Elevator
5

Private grain
elevators
(Ogilvie,
Five Roses)

IN 1945, THE PORT OF MONTRÉAL WAS DRIVEN BY THE CONSTANT NEEDS OF THE MANUFACTURING AND GRAIN INDUSTRIES. COAL, STILL COMMONLY USED FOR FUEL, WAS UNLOADED ON BICKERDIKE QUAY. GRAIN ELEVATORS 1, 2 AND 5, WHOSE CONVEYOR GALLERIES WERE BUILT ON TOP OF THE STORAGE SHEDS, RAN AT FULL CAPACITY. THE LACHINE CANAL, WITH A DOUBLE SET OF LOCKS AT ITS ENTRANCE, WAS THE ONLY NAVIGABLE WATERWAY PROVIDING ACCESS TO THE WEST. THE GREEN CIRCLES INDICATE THE BUILDINGS THAT STILL EXIST TODAY.

Cold Storage
Warehouse

Bickerdike
Pier

Windmill
Point
Basin

STEAM COAL

How did it *work* ?

Transferring grain from a boat to an elevator

Marine Tower

Boat

If we found ourselves back around 1960 and a long grain carrier had just docked at the pier used by grain elevator 1 (Conveyor Quay) in the port of Montréal, two marine towers would go immediately into action to remove its heavy cargo of grain.

Each tower worked in the same way as the first floating elevators—even though electricity had replaced steam as an energy source.

1 The *marine leg* would emerge from its compartment and be extended into the hold.

2 Its bucket conveyor would start to work, lifting the grain up.

3 The grain would flow through a chute and onto a *conveyor* (a moving belt), itself housed in a tunnel running under the surface of the quay.

4 At the end of the tunnel another bucket conveyor would lift the grain up again and drop it onto a scale for weighing.

5 The load of grain would then be moved into the elevator. It would remain there in storage until it was loaded onto another boat (or onto a railway car). The grain would then be poured through movable spouts located along the conveyor's overhead gallery.

If the grain from the west was heading for a Montréal flour-mill—Ogilvie or another one located on the banks of the Lachine Canal—it would be unloaded from the boat right into the company's grain elevator.

Marine Tower

Boat

Scale

Elevator

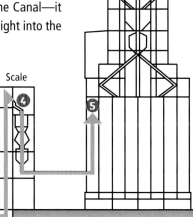

66

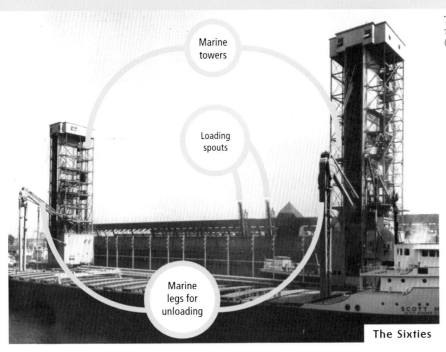

Marine towers

Loading spouts

Marine legs for unloading

The Sixties

ONE OF THE TWO MARINE TOWERS CAN STILL BE SEEN IN THE OLD PORT OF MONTRÉAL. IT IS KNOWN AS "CONVEYOR TOWER". MANY OF ITS ORIGINAL COMPONENTS ARE STILL THERE: THE MARINE LEG ON ITS BASE, SEVERAL BUCKETS ON THE BELT, THE HOPPER THROUGH WHICH THE GRAIN FLOWED ON ITS WAY TO ELEVATOR 1 VIA AN UNDERGROUND CONVEYOR, AND THE ROLL-UP DOOR THAT COVERED THE LEG'S COMPARTMENT WHEN THE LEG WAS NOT IN USE.

THIS PHOTO ALSO SHOWS TWO MECHANISMS ADDED TO MAKE IT POSSIBLE TO COMPLETELY EMPTY THE HOLDS OF GRAIN: A CRANE WHICH INTRODUCED A MECHANICAL LOADER CAPABLE OF REACHING AREAS UNATTAINABLE BY THE CONVEYOR AND A VACUUM PIPE WHICH COULD PICK UP ANY GRAIN REMAINING IN HARD TO REACH PLACES. THESE MECHANISMS THUS REPLACED THE SHOVELLERS WHOSE JOB IT HAD BEEN TO PUSH THE GRAIN TOWARD THE CONVEYOR.

Roll-up door

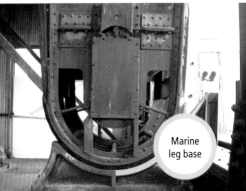

Marine leg base

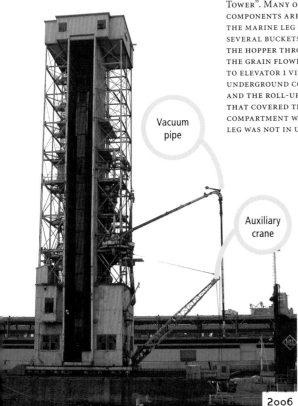

Vacuum pipe

Auxiliary crane

2006

Buckets

Hopper

Toward the underground conveyor

1910

2006

Then and now

ON THE LEFT
MANY GALLERIES WERE
LOCATED ON TOP OF THE
SHEDS IN THE PORT.
THE OUTLINES OF GRAIN
ELEVATORS A AND B
APPEAR TO THE RIGHT OF
BONSECOURS MARKET AND
(FURTHER WEST) OF CITY
HALL AS IT LOOKED BEFORE
THE 1922 FIRE.

ON THE RIGHT
CONVEYOR TOWER,
A SIGNIFICANT REMINDER OF
THE GRAIN TRANSSHIPPING
SYSTEM THAT WAS THE
PORT'S PRIDE AND GLORY.

Until 1920, grain was unloaded from the railcars with shovels: a team of two shovellers could empty about fifteen railcars a day. Then, to speed up the work, engineer John S. Metcalf developed a device located inside the elevator that made it possible to empty the railcars directly. The Metcalf car dumper (installed on a track that ran through the elevator) could lift and tilt the car from front to back as well as from side to side.

A single car dumper unloaded nearly seven cars an hour: five times the output! Of course, shovellers were still needed to empty the cargo completely. In elevator 2, for example, four car dumpers on as many tracks could mechanically unload 28 cars per hour. This is how it worked:

1 When the railcar was tilted, the grain would flow into a hopper.

2 A bucket conveyor would lift the grain from the bottom of the hopper . . .

3 . . . to the top of the tower. From there . . .

4 . . . the grain would flow into another hopper, where it would be weighed.

5 The batch would then be poured onto a belt conveyor and carried to the storage elevator . . .

6 . . . unless it was to go to a shipping elevator, where it would be loaded onto a train . . .

7 . . . or onto a boat through the overhead conveyor galleries.

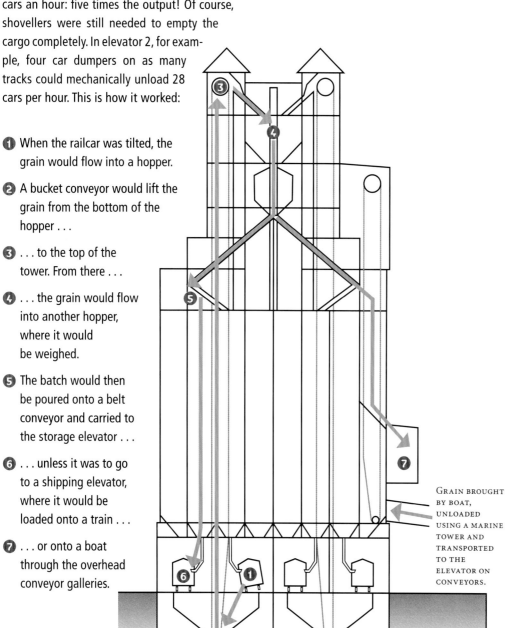

GRAIN BROUGHT BY BOAT, UNLOADED USING A MARINE TOWER AND TRANSPORTED TO THE ELEVATOR ON CONVEYORS.

GRAIN ELEVATOR 5 STILL
HAS TRACKS RUNNING
THROUGH IT—UNUSED
SINCE THE ELEVATOR
STOPPED OPERATING IN 1995.

ON THE LEFT
THE METCALF CAR DUMPER
IN ACTION. THIS SYSTEM
WOULD FALL INTO DISUSE
WITH THE DEVELOPMENT
OF COVERED HOPPER CARS
DESIGNED FOR TRANSPOR-
TING GRAIN, AS THESE WERE
EQUIPPED WITH HOPPERS
THAT COULD BE OPENED AT
THE BOTTOM, ALLOWING THE
CARGO SIMPLY TO FLOW OUT.

Elevator 1

IN 1902, THE PORT
AUTHORITIES BEGAN
BUILDING ELEVATOR 1,
WHILE THE GRAND
TRUNK RAILWAY (THE
FORERUNNER OF
CANADIAN NATIONAL)
BUILT THE STEEL
SECTION OF ELEVATOR 5.

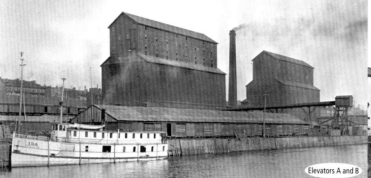

Elevators A and B

Elevator 5

The magnificent grain elevators

There is no structure that better exemplifies how important the port of Montréal was in the transshipment of grain than the grain elevator. Inside, the grain was hoisted from the bottom to the top using impressive bucket conveyors, the heads of which projected above the rooftop, each in its own gabled tower.

The first elevators—built between 1885 and 1887, by the Canadian Pacific Railway—were made of wood and looked like the elevators found across the Canadian prairies. But as of 1902, the Commissioners began the construction of the first modern grain elevator, known as elevator 1.

That same year, the Grand Trunk Railway, the rival of the Canadian Pacific Railway, leased a piece of land on Windmill Point from the port authorities and began building elevator 5—known at the time as the Grand Trunk elevator. The Harbour Commissioners took it over in 1923 and gradually enlarged it to its current size.

Soon, grain and cereals took the lead among the commodities being shipped through the port. Another elevator was needed. As a result, in 1912, elevator 2 was erected. The builders took a chance on a new material: for the first time anywhere, a building of this kind was constructed entirely of reinforced concrete, including the storage bins. A photo of the giant structure appeared not only in international engineering publications, but also in art magazines. Le Corbusier himself saw the grain elevator as a symbol of modern architecture.

But grain transshipping continued to expand . . . existing elevators were extended and then, in 1924, elevator 3 was added further east. Four years later, the port's storage capacity reached over 15 million bushels. Finally, in 1963, elevator 4 was added, also in the east end.

With the passage of time, however, grain shipping activity in the port of Montréal began to decline, for a variety of reasons. From 1959 onward, the St. Lawrence Seaway allowed ocean-going vessels to sail all the way to the head of the Great Lakes to load their grain. There were more self-unloading ships. And as more and more Canadian wheat was being exported to Asia, the port of Vancouver took on greater importance. In 1978, elevator 2 was demolished, as part of the plan to modernize the port facilities. In 1983, the Old Port of Montréal Corporation began to tear down elevator 1 to create a wider "window on the river", as desired by the public. In 1995, elevator 5 ceased operations.

Today, several elevators owned by private companies still operate in Montréal—one of which is elevator 3. Elevator 4 is the only one for which the port has responsibility; its grain handling operation is completely mechanized. In the Old Port, however, Conveyor Quay and its remaining marine tower are reminders of Montréal's golden age of grain. The same is true of the remains of the pier beside elevator 2 and the marine tower in Bonsecours Basin. The remains of the elevator itself are now covered by grass, but they were visible for a time across from Bonsecours Market. The idea of developing the site by evoking in an original way the huge building that once stood there has not yet been abandoned. But the most impressive survivor of the era is without doubt elevator 5, at the westernmost end of the port. Because its structures and equipment have been maintained, it is the most complete remaining example of the transshipping system. Some of its facilities are still used by neighbouring flour mills.

Nowadays, grain elevator redevelopment projects can be found all over the world. To make this kind of project happen, people have to pool their ideas and demonstrate the sort of imagination and innovation that built these giants in the first place. The question of what to do with elevator 5 has already caused much debate and given rise to many proposals . . . stay tuned.

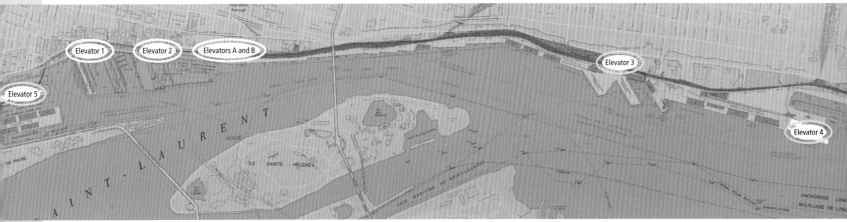

THE PORT OF MONTRÉAL HAD
AS MANY AS FIVE ELEVATORS
OPERATING AT ONCE. WHEN IT
OPENED IN 1963, ELEVATOR 4
WAS ON THE CUTTING EDGE OF
TECHNOLOGY. IT IS STILL IN USE.

AT THE PARIS WORLD'S
FAIR IN 1937, THE
GRAIN ELEVATOR'S
ARCHITECTURAL STYLE
WAS USED AS A MODEL FOR
THE CANADIAN PAVILION.

1912

ELEVATOR 2
THE CONSTRUCTION OF THIS
ELEVATOR BEGAN IN 1912, ACROSS
FROM BONSECOURS MARKET.
A SYMBOL OF MODERN
ARCHITECTURE, IN THE OPINION
OF LE CORBUSIER, IT WAS
DEMOLISHED BY IMPLOSION IN 1978.

BELOW, THE REMAINS OF
ELEVATOR 2 WERE VISIBLE TO
THE PUBLIC FROM 1992 TO 2003.

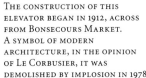

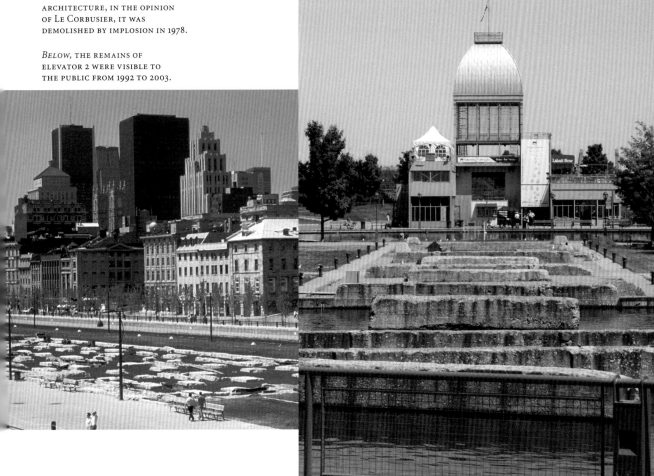

THE REMAINS OF THE
PIER AND MARINE TOWER
THAT SERVED ELEVATOR
2 ARE STILL VISIBLE IN
BONSECOURS BASIN.

ELEVATOR 5
DESIGNATED AS A
RECOGNIZED FEDERAL
HERITAGE BUILDING,
THIS ABANDONED
ELEVATOR, TOWERING
OVER THE OLD PORT AND
THE LACHINE CANAL, IS A
MAJESTIC SYMBOL OF THE
MAJOR ROLE PLAYED BY
THE PORT OF MONTRÉAL
IN GRAIN TRANSSHIPPING.
THE AESTHETIC VALUE OF
THIS KIND OF BUILDING,
WHILE NOT IMMEDIATELY
OBVIOUS TODAY, WAS ONCE
CONSIDERABLE. ELEVATORS
WERE DEEMED TO BE
MONUMENTS OF MODERN
ARCHITECTURE IN THE
FIRST HALF OF THE
TWENTIETH CENTURY.
THEIR HERITAGE VALUE
LIES AS MUCH IN THE
MATERIALS USED TO BUILD
THEM—STEEL AND
CONCRETE, NEW AT THE
TIME—AS IN THE CUSTOM-
DESIGNED MECHANICAL
SYSTEMS THAT MAKE EACH
ELEVATOR UNIQUE.

The cold storage warehouse and its plant

Grain was not the only commodity shipped through the port of Montréal—far from it. Perishable goods—meat, cheese, fruit, vegetables—also arrived on the quays and had to be stored in suitable conditions while waiting to be delivered.

The cold storage warehouse was opened in 1922, when grain shipping activity was at its peak. Its architecture was particularly elaborate and the job of designing it was given to the company of John S. Metcalf, the engineer who had designed the first large elevators in the port, as well as their conveyor systems.

The cold storage warehouse was built on concrete pillars called pedestal piles, consisting of a metal tube drilled into the ground and filled with concrete. The pillars, measuring about 30 centimetres in diameter, had to have a weight-bearing capacity of forty tonnes. Tests showed they could support up to 65 tonnes! The drilling contract was awarded to the MacArthur Concrete Pile and Foundation Co. of Montréal.

The process used to keep the warehouse cool, installed by R. Percy Sims, was at the forefront of technology. A brine solution of calcium chloride, cooled to an extremely low temperature using a process involving the expansion of anhydrous ammonia, kept the building cold. Ammonia compressors made by Linde were powered by electricity.

The equipment, set up in duplicate to guarantee a supply of coolant in case of a breakdown, was housed in a building next to the warehouse. This building echoed the architectural style of the warehouse and was also built on pillars. The refrigeration plant (then called the "Power House") also housed a machine that could produce up to five tonnes of ice per day in 45 kilogram blocks, used by the port authorities for tugboats (whose crews had to be able to keep their food cold) and for the stores, among other uses. The building also had an electric station for servicing the new electric trains.

Not far from the warehouse, a well provided a steady supply of 4° C water for the system. This is the temperature of a modern refrigerator, which made the cooling process easier, as well as making it possible to preserve meat, fruit and vegetables. The well's considerable depth—372 metres—was often emphasized by the authorities when they sang the praises of the port facilities.

There were other privately run cold storage warehouses in the area, such as the Cherrier cold storage warehouse (1896-1980) at the intersection of Saint Vincent and Saint Amable streets. Another warehouse that was just as large as the one in the port of Montréal stood just to the north on Saint Antoine, between Amherst and Montcalm streets: Montréal Refrigerating and Storage. It was demolished in 1996 after a series of accidents befell some squatters living in the stripped-down building.

The cold storage warehouse in the port was used until 1978. As its refrigeration plant had stopped operating in 1968 (it was demolished in 1976), an electric power station had been installed and one of the reservoirs designed to supply water in case of fire was used to store the cooling solution. Designated as a Recognized federal heritage building in 1996, the Old Port of Montréal Corporation transferred it to a private investor a few years ago; it has been converted into a luxurious residential complex.

A HUGE FRIDGE
USING LINDE COMPRESSORS (BELOW) INSTALLED IN THE PLANT, THE COLD STORAGE WAREHOUSE ENSURED THAT PERISHABLE GOODS WERE PRESERVED WHILE IN TRANSIT.

1924

THE REFRIGERATION PLANT HOUSED A MACHINE THAT COULD PRODUCE 45-KILOGRAM BLOCKS OF ICE.

1954

2006

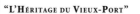

1932

"L'HÉRITAGE DU VIEUX-PORT"
WHEN THE COLD-STORAGE WAREHOUSE WAS CONVERTED INTO A RESIDENTIAL COMPLEX, THE EXTERIOR SHELL AS WELL AS THE FOUR TOWERS THAT CONTAINED THE FIRE PROTECTION SYSTEM'S CISTERNS AND THE BRINE RESERVOIR WERE PRESERVED. TODAY THEY HOUSE PRESTIGIOUS CONDOMINIUM APARTMENTS.

THE PORT POLICE STATION, AS IT LOOKED AFTER IT WAS GUTTED IN 1985.

The police station

There has been a police force in the port of Montréal ever since 1851! In 1924 the force moved into the "New Wharf Office Building", built the previous year by the Montréal firm Collet Frères, based on plans by architect Théodose Daoust (1867-1937). The building housed (aside from one cell!) technical and administrative services: the harbour master's office (ships' receiving and accounting), a store, a weigh station, a blacksmith's shop, a tinsmithy, a garage . . .

It appears that the idea was to create a handsome building. Visible from the entrance to the port, given its location at the junction of Victoria Pier (today Clock Tower Quay) and the high-level quays (at the eastern end of the current promenade), it was built in the Italian Renaissance style and covered with buff-coloured glazed bricks that contrasted sharply with the concrete and steel of the sur-

rounding structures—as well as with the red brick and more classical architecture of the only other administrative building in the port at the time, near elevator 1. It also had a high tower where the water supply hoses for steam boats were dried out, giving it the look of a fire station, and a second smaller tower that housed a stairwell leading to a look-out where, as in the other tower, there stood a flagpole.

When the Old Port of Montréal took over the site, the port police were moved temporarily into shed 16. Some years later, in 1985, the Corporation had the police station gutted, with a view to restoring it at a later date. However, after having been neglected for so many years, the structure was already in a very bad state of repair. Despite its having been designated as a Recognized federal heritage building in 1996, the decision was finally made in 2003 to tear the lovely building down.

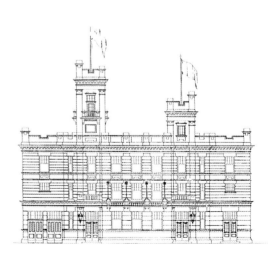

THE POLICE STATION STOOD AT THE ENTRANCE TO CLOCK TOWER QUAY.

WHEN THE POLICE STATION WAS TORN DOWN, SHEDS 22 AND 23, LOCATED BETWEEN THE COLD STORAGE WAREHOUSE AND SHED 16, BECAME VISIBLE FROM THE OLD PORT PROMENADE.

2002

2006

1878

1887-1888

2006

Then and now

In 1871, the first railway track was laid on the quays of the port of Montréal. In 1884, a second track was added. After 1910, the number of tracks increased on the higher level quays and piers. Now there are between one and three tracks connecting the quays of the port with other locations in the Old Port. Note as well the stone wall in the left photographs to which was added a blockade, seen in the lower photograph.

The clock towers

Three buildings with a tower and a clock can be seen from the Old Port. Two of these are located on the north side of De la Commune Street just outside the Old Port's perimeter. A third building is located at the downstream edge of the Old Port.

At the time these were being built, many Montrealers could not afford a watch. Being able to tell time from a distance was absolutely essential, both for managing work in a factory and for keeping things moving in the port—so much so that it is said workers arrived late if the clock on the clock tower stopped! The popularity of clock towers was revived in the twentieth century, notably on the Molson Brewery Building located further east and still clearly visible from the Old Port.

The Commissioners Building

Of all the buildings connected to port activities that can still be seen in Old Montréal, the most impressive is without a doubt the Commissioners Building at 357 De la Commune Street West. Built between 1874 and 1878, the building was planned by a consortium of architects including John William Hopkins, Daniel B. Wily and Alexander Cowper Hutchison. The building would house the offices of the Montréal Harbour Commission.

Aside from the mayor of Montréal, who was a member by virtue of his office, the Commissioners were comprised of representatives from the Montréal Chamber of Commerce, the grain exchange and shipping companies. The Montréal Port Authority, the entity that now manages the commercial port from the Cité du Havre, is still made up of government officials and business people from the area.

The current owner of the Commissioners Building, Terra Incognita Inc., thanks to the Daniel Langlois foundation, carried out significant renovation work in 2000 and 2001, with the result that this magnificent piece of architecture, neglected for over three decades, was not only able to survive, but also to regain its former spendour.

WITH A CLOCK ON ITS DOME, THE COMMISSIONERS BUILDING STILL TOWERS OVER THE HARBOURFRONT.

THE HARBOUR COMMISSIONERS IN 1888 THE BUILDING'S ORIGINAL DOORS, BEARING THE COAT OF ARMS OF THE MONTRÉAL HARBOUR COMMISSION, ARE NOW ON DISPLAY IN THE EXHIBIT ROOM OF THE MONTRÉAL PORT AUTHORITY OFFICES IN CITÉ DU HAVRE.

ON THE SIDE FACING DE LA COMMUNE STREET IS A MONUMENT TO JOHN YOUNG, WHO BECAME PRESIDENT OF THE MONTRÉAL HARBOUR COMMISSION IN 1853. THIS STATUE ONCE STOOD IN FRONT OF THE ROYAL INSURANCE BUILDING.

THE INSCRIPTION "H & A ALLAN" IS STILL SEEN ON THE FAÇADE OF THE ALLAN BUILDING ON D'YOUVILLE STREET.

The Edmonstone, Allan & Co. Building

Just to the right of the Commissioners Building, on the waterfront overlooking the port, there is another great building tied in with the history of the port. Also designed by architect John William Hopkins, it was built in 1858 to house the offices of the Edmonstone, Allan & Co. shipping company.

The "Allan Building" was restored in 1983 by the Old Port of Montréal Corporation, which has had its offices there ever since.

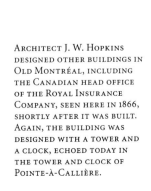

ARCHITECT J. W. HOPKINS DESIGNED OTHER BUILDINGS IN OLD MONTRÉAL, INCLUDING THE CANADIAN HEAD OFFICE OF THE ROYAL INSURANCE COMPANY, SEEN HERE IN 1866, SHORTLY AFTER IT WAS BUILT. AGAIN, THE BUILDING WAS DESIGNED WITH A TOWER AND A CLOCK, ECHOED TODAY IN THE TOWER AND CLOCK OF POINTE-À-CALLIÈRE.

The Clock Tower

Between 1919 and 1922 an elegant white tower in the Beaux-Arts style was built at the downstream end of the port. It had many purposes: it marked the entrance to the port, served as a commemorative monument to the men of the merchant navy lost at sea in World War I, told the time from the top of its 45-metre height and, thanks to its wall and turret, hid the nearby sheds.

Like that of Big Ben in London, which was the inspiration for architect Paul Leclaire, the tower has a clock face on each of its four sides. Passersby and sailors could thus see the time from wherever they were and from as far away as Sherbrooke Street. Space was also included to house a bell to ring the hours, but the bell was never installed.

The symbol of the Old Port, the Clock Tower has been home to an interpretative centre and an observatory since 1980. Restored in 1984 and 1988, and designated a "Classified federal heritage building" in 1996, it continues to host commemorative ceremonies.

THE CLOCK TOWER'S HIGH PRECISION CLOCK MECHANISM WAS BUILT IN ENGLAND IN 1922 BY GILLETT AND JOHNSTON, THE ROYAL CLOCKMAKER WHO, AS THE LETTERHEAD ON THE OFFER OF SERVICES ADDRESSED TO THE PORT OF MONTRÉAL INDICATES, MADE THE DEVICE THAT MAKES BIG BEN RING. IT HAS A SET OF COGS THAT CHANGE THE VERTICAL MOTION OF THE COUNTERWEIGHT INTO THE ROTARY MOTION OF THE HANDS ON THE FOUR CLOCK FACES. AN AUTOMATIC WINDING SYSTEM DRIVEN BY AN ELECTRIC MOTOR WAS INSTALLED IN THE 1950S. FOR THE PAST 15 YEARS, THE OLD PORT OF MONTRÉAL HAS ENTRUSTED THE MAINTENANCE OF THIS DELICATE MECHANISM TO DANIEL PELLETIER, ONE OF THE FEW ARTISAN CLOCKMAKERS STILL POSSESSING THE REQUIRED SKILLS.

EQUALLY VISIBLE FROM
THE CITY, THE PORT AND
THE RIVER, THE CLOCK
TOWER CONTINUES
TO TELL TIME FOR
MONTREALERS.

As we have seen, the historic buildings of the Old Port of Montréal speak volumes about the leading role played by the city and its port in the development of Quebec and Canada. In 25 years, under the direction of the Old Port of Montréal Corporation, the remaining structures have been restored with respect for the past. But the restoration has also revitalized the area in countless ways, transforming it today into an urban park designed for recreation, tourism and culture. So let's set a course for the Old Port, bustling with activity . . . then and now.

A port humming with activity

The "old" port was once a very busy place: full of labourers and longshoremen at work, home to sailors passing through, dreamt of by immigrants in search of a better life in North America.

The Old Port today is as busy as ever. It is true that there is less shipping activity; no one comes to greet the Prince of Wales's fleet any more, and new arrivals choose the airport over the port. But people still come here to walk, stroll, read—work—, keep in shape, admire the fireworks, visit an exhibition, attend a performance, celebrate Canada Day. In fact, more people come here today than ever before. Several million people visit the site every year. And within this human tapestry, there are hundreds of thousands of lives whose destinies crossed paths in this place . . .

IN THE LAST TWENTY-FIVE YEARS, THE OLD PORT HAS CHANGED FROM A COMMERCIAL AND INDUSTRIAL SITE INTO A PLACE FOR RECREATION AND TOURISM, WHERE MAJOR EVENTS AND PERFORMANCES ARE REGULARLY SCHEDULED. THIS FESTIVE TRADITION GOES BACK A LONG WAY, ONE EXAMPLE OF THIS BEING THE CONSTRUCTION, IN 1860, OF AN ARCH OF TRIUMPH ON THE QUAYS TO HONOUR THE PRINCE OF WALES WHEN HE CAME TO INAUGURATE THE VICTORIA BRIDGE.

A port waiting to be built

The liveliness of the Old Port of Montréal to-day should serve as a reminder of those who designed, built and regularly passed through the port in days gone by. Credit goes to two builders named John, both of whom were driving forces in the development of Montréal.

THE STATUE OF JOHN YOUNG, INITIALLY LOCATED IN FRONT OF THE ROYAL INSURANCE BUILDING, NOW STANDS IN FRONT OF THE EDMONSTONE, ALLAN & CO. BUILDING.

Developing the port: John Young and John Kennedy

THE SON OF A COOPER, THE TIRELESS AND PERSISTENT JOHN YOUNG (1811-1878) HAD AN EXCEPTIONAL CAREER IN A NUMBER OF FIELDS.

John Young, president of the Montréal Harbour Commission for many years, more than earned the right to survey the former port from atop his bronze statue, in front of 333 De la Commune Street West. In 1850, under his guidance, the deepening of the channel between Montréal and Quebec City was begun—a task that had just been assigned to the commissioners. This was a colossal construction project of critical importance: dredging a channel to allow oceangoing ships to sail through the shallow waters of Lake St. Pierre turned Montréal from a river port into an international port.

While trying his hand at politics, notably as a member of Parliament for a Montréal riding and as Commissioner of Public Works, Young was also a clever businessman. He was involved in railway companies as well as in other businesses, such as the Montréal Warehousing Company Flour Mills and the St. Gabriel Hydraulic Company, established at the St. Gabriel Lock on the Lachine Canal.

SIR JOHN KENNEDY (1838-1921).

At the beginning of the twentieth century, John Kennedy took the helm of the port as chief engineer, with the intention of modernizing the site's infrastructure. Appointed in 1875, just as serious discussions on the need to re-examine the facilities were getting underway, he was in charge of raising the quays and building the large piers—Alexandra, King Edward, Jacques Cartier, Victoria, Mackay—, the flood wall, the storage sheds and the elevators. These were projects that would take 44 years to complete and that he would continue to supervise even after losing his sight in 1907. He became a "Sir" in 1916 when knighted by King George V, in recognition of his work in the port of Montréal.

RIGHT
IN THE BACKGROUND, THE OLD PORT AND THE CITY. IN THE FOREGROUND, THE POWERFUL SELF-PROPELLED FLOATING CRANE VM/S HERCULES, BUILT IN 1962 TO SERVE AS A GATE LIFTER FOR THE CANADIAN LOCKS IN THE ST. LAWRENCE SEAWAY. TODAY ITS SERVICES ARE OFTEN REQUESTED BY LOCAL COMPANIES TO LOAD OR UNLOAD HEAVY CARGO. IN THE CENTRE, BICKERDIKE QUAY, WHOSE SHEDS WERE PARTIALLY TORN DOWN IN RECENT YEARS TO MAKE WAY FOR CONTAINERS.

1915

Wielding pick and shovel: the labourers

John Kennedy had big dreams for the port. At the beginning of the twentieth century, to bring his ambitious plans to fruition, an average of 1,000 to 1,500 workers were hired each year. Teams were kept busy all over the site: in administration, in the sheds, in the workshops, on the railway tracks, maintaining the locomotives, building elevators ... In 1912, when elevator 2 was being built, there were 2,393 labourers at work!

Where did all these men live? The annual Harbour Commissioners' reports don't tell us. However, it is likely they lived near their workplace, in Griffintown, downtown (now Old Montréal) or a little to the east, in the Quebec suburb. Since work in the port was seasonal at the time, some labourers rented rooms on nearby streets for as long as they were working. In the winter they went back to their villages, scattered along on the shores of the St. Lawrence.

Then, as the port shifted eastward, so did they, to neighbourhoods in the new areas of Hochelaga-Maisonneuve. From the 1950s onward, more extensive public transit and more cars meant that workers could live further away.

Working with saw and anvil: the carpenters and blacksmiths

The workforce was not just made up of labourers with no particular qualifications. Many skilled tradesmen were required. Carpenters built everything made of wood (the main construction material at the time), from the structure of the quays to the frames of the temporary sheds. In the mechanical workshops, blacksmiths repaired most of the equipment and cast parts (including replacement parts) for dredgers, locomotives and elevators. When the workshops were taken down after the port authorities started to use external suppliers, several of the wooden moulds used for cast metal parts were saved.

THIS ILLUSTRATION, DATING FROM THE NINETEENTH CENTURY, SHOWS WORKERS VIGOROUSLY CLEARING AWAY ICE IN THE SPRING. IN THE PHOTOS, TAKEN AT A LATER DATE, THEY ARE BUSY BUILDING ELEVATORS AND PERMANENT SHEDS ON THE QUAYS, WHICH BY THEN HAD BEEN RAISED.

1920

Table of Employees in 1916

	Maximum	Average
Maintenance of Harbour	123	89
Police	45	43
Construction of wharves, tracks, etc.	362	275
Harbour Yard, carpenters, blacksmiths, etc.	27	26
Sawmill and Timber boom	30	25
Round House*, machinists, etc.	21	18
Machine Shop	89	71
Shipyard	50	47
Dredging Fleet, dredges, tugs, etc., crews	201	175
Construction West Extension elevator 1	135	95
Operation: Elevator 1	64	46
Operation: Elevator 2	89	69
Conveyor Galleries	42	40
Floating Elevators	10	8
Shovellers	32	22
Electrical Department, Hoists, etc.	27	25
Traffic Department	103	88
TOTAL	**1450**	**1162**

This table, an excerpt from the Port of Montréal's 1916 annual report, shows that the bulk of the workers were employed to build the quays and the railway tracks, as well as to extend elevator 1. The number of men assigned to these tasks varied over the years, while in other categories the numbers varied little. The dredging team was especially large. However, it was the grain transshipping sector that employed the largest numbers of workers.

*Roundhouse: a series of workshops built in a circle around a central track; when this track was rotated, the locomotive could be driven into a workshop for servicing.

Nearly half of the dredging and towing team is seen in this photo taken in 1910.

Workers at the controls of dredgers and cranes are busy enlarging Jacques Cartier Quay. In the background, Mackay Pier (now the Cité du Havre), where dredgers and tugboats requiring repairs were moored.

1919

Surfacing the port: the track layers and pavers

In 1907 and 1908, the port was literally covered over with railway tracks and paving stones! The hundreds of employees assigned to this task were almost all Italian, as Canadians did not rush to sign up for this kind of work.

The tracks were laid by teams, each one managed by a general foreman with three sub-foremen and made up of track layers, tampers (who laid the "ballast") and labourers. Ballast consisted of crushed gravel used to fill in the spaces between the tracks and the ties to make the trains run more smoothly. Boats at the time used this material as ballast; hence the name was used in track laying as well.

On the quays and between the tracks, concrete mixers, pavers, grouters and labourers replaced wooden boards and macadam with paving stones, first made from slag and later from granite. Finally, asphalt was laid between 1950 and 1960. This was a noticeable improvement for vehicles but also for everyone's ears, although the cars bumping along over the paving stones did not make anything like the racket of the hundreds of carriages and horse-drawn vehicles with metal-rimmed wheels in the early years of the century!

When the Old Port and Old Montréal were redeveloped, the original paving was preserved in some areas and completely replaced in others. As a result, it is still possible to see paving stones made of pink or grey granite and others made of slag—with a glazed surface, blue or green in colour—, brick or concrete.

Managing the tracks: the switchmen

In 1907, the railway tracks laid in the port by the Grand Trunk since 1871 became the direct responsibility of the Commissioners. They created a Department of Transport, purchased locomotives and began to hire employees.

One of the most specialized railway jobs was that of the switchman. This critical and delicate task, which involved directing each train onto the right track, became even more important as new tracks were added. In some places, around the elevators for example, there were as many as ten parallel tracks!

Other workers looked after the steam trains that ran all over the port; these were driven right into the elevators and the cold storage warehouse for unloading and loading. Engineers drove the locomotives, with firemen stoking the boiler on each one.

Teams of mechanics took turns ensuring that the heavy machinery was kept in good repair. In 1923, electric locomotives began to be used in the port, and electricians joined the workforce.

IN THE TWENTIETH CENTURY, BOTH RAILWAY AND ROAD TRAFFIC IN THE PORT INCREASED. WORKERS WERE KEPT BUSY LAYING THE TRACKS AND PAVING THE ROAD SURFACES.

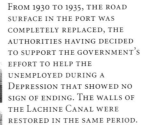

From 1930 to 1935, the road surface in the port was completely replaced, the authorities having decided to support the government's effort to help the unemployed during a Depression that showed no sign of ending. The walls of the Lachine Canal were restored in the same period.

A visitor on foot will have the best view of the patchwork of old and new paving stones on Quay 1, between Locks 1 and 2 on the Lachine Canal.

Young boys carried drinking water all over the port, in two pails attached to a yoke planted firmly on their shoulders.

Handling cargo: the longshoremen

Today, as in the past, longshoremen make up the largest group of workers in the Port of Montréal: their union has roughly 1,000 members. When the port was at its peak, in the 1920s and 1930s, no fewer than 3,700 workers belonged to it—and in reality there were even more, since at the time you didn't have to belong to the union to work. In fact, from 1940 to 1966, non-unionized workers outnumbered union members.

The opening of the St. Lawrence Seaway, which put an end to the need for break-bulk cargo handling and led to increasingly mechanized operations, resulted in a sizeable decline in the workforce. Nonetheless, longshoremen are still the only port workers licensed to carry out work related to loading and unloading goods in transit other than grain.

The lives of these workers have changed a great deal since the first half of the twentieth century, as described by writer Jean-Jules Richard in 1970. For a long time, working in teams, they loaded and unloaded the boats manually, moving goods into sheds, onto railcars, carts, trucks . . . while also handling passenger baggage. Today, the grappling hook, the classic symbol of the longshoreman, no longer hangs over their shoulders or from their belts, although it is still part of the union logo. It has been replaced by machinery.

Starting early in the nineteenth century, the first Irish immigrants entered the profession. Some of their descendants now work as inspectors—while the majority of longshoremen today are Francophones, whose families hailed from the Gaspé and the shores of the St. Lawrence in the 1880s, like so many others, lured from the countryside to the big city.

Syndicat des Débardeurs du Port de Montréal
SCFP Section locale 375

AT THE VERY BEGINNING OF THE TWENTIETH CENTURY, THE LONGSHOREMEN'S DEMANDS WERE TAKEN UP BY AN ACCREDITED UNION THAT ACTED AS A KIND OF PLACEMENT AGENCY FOR SHIPPING COMPANIES. THE MONTRÉAL LONGSHOREMEN'S UNION, LOCAL 375, WAS AFFILIATED WITH THE INTERNATIONAL LONGSHOREMEN'S ASSOCIATION BETWEEN 1902 AND 1907 AND AGAIN FROM 1935 TO 1990. IT IS NOW AFFILIATED WITH THE CANADIAN UNION OF PUBLIC EMPLOYEES.

LOADING TIMBER ONTO THE *TURRETT AGE*.

1895

LES DEBARDEURS SYNDIQUES DU PORT DE MONTREAL FONT CONSTRUIRE UN EDIFICE

22-3-1913

Le Syndicat des Débardeurs de Montréal aura bientôt son propre édifice. Il a chargé son architecte, M. Charles Chaussée, d'en dessiner les plans et les entrepreneurs devront envoyer leurs soumissions au plus tard le 25 de ce mois, à midi. Le nouvel édifice sera construit rue du Champ-de-Mars, près de la rue Berri, et aura trois étages, en brique. Il sera complètement à l'épreuve du feu. La façade sera ornée de frontons et de corniches en cuivre.

C'est la première organisation ouvrière de Montréal qui se fait construire un édifice et l'on peut dire que c'est là un bel exemple qu'elle donne aux autres.

Le rez-de-chaussée sera occupé par une vaste salle de réunion que les autres associations pourront louer. Les autres étages seront occupés par des bureaux pour les hommes d'affaires.

Il est entendu que tout doit être terminé pour la fin du mois de juin au plus tard.

L'installation sera des plus modernes. L'on y trouvera de spacieuses chambres de toilette, des voûtes de sûreté et tout ce qui peut donner le confort.

Les murs et les plafonds seront recouverts de tôle.

PLANS DE L'EDIFICE DU SYNDICAT DES DEBARDEURS que l'on va prochainement faire construire rue du Champ-de-Mars. — C'est la première des organisations ouvrières de Montréal qui se fait construire un édifice à elle. — Les plans ont été faits par l'architecte Charles Chaussée, 1975 avenue du Parc.

Around 1900

_G_ood question! What do you think you're doing? That's the best we've got! What's it for? That depends on what you mean. It's tough nowadays with all the machinery! I guess it's sort of an ornament and a jewel. As much an ornament as a vice, as much a badge of pride as a jewel. Pride's a rare thing on the docks and you wear it like a piece of jewellery, but it can tear a man apart, just like any vice. What do you think you're doing? A vice, that's right, because someday they're going to come and say: The only ones working are the vicious ones. Let machines do the work. What are you doing? Are you crazy?

JEAN-JULES RICHARD, 1970 (free translation)

UNLOADING ONTO
THE QUAYS.

AS JEAN-JULES RICHARD HAD
FORESEEN, MACHINERY IS NOW
FOUND EVERYWHERE IN THE
PORT OF MONTRÉAL. IN
ADDITION, GOODS ARE MORE
AND MORE OFTEN TRANSPORTED
IN CONTAINERS RATHER THAN
IN THE BARRELS, CRATES OR
BUNDLES TYPICAL OF
TRANSSHIPPING IN THE PAST. IN
2006, OVER 45% OF THE GOODS
TRANSITING THROUGH THE
PORT WERE CONTAINERIZED.

BETWEEN 1940 AND 1980,
THE LONGSHOREMEN
WORKED IN TEAMS OF 18
MEN, AS SEEN IN THIS
PHOTO, WHERE A NUMBER
OF THEM PROUDLY CARRY
THEIR GRAPPLING HOOK
OVER THEIR SHOULDER.
LATER, THERE WERE 12
AND THEN 8. THE ONLY
LONGSHOREMEN NOW
WORKING IN THE OLD
PORT AREA WORK IN THE
PASSENGER TERMINAL ON
ALEXANDRA QUAY, UNDER
THE MANAGEMENT OF THE
PORT AUTHORITIES.

LONGSHOREMEN AT WORK AROUND 1896
REMEMBER THAT IN THE NINETEENTH CENTURY THE STORAGE SHEDS ON THE QUAYS HAD TO BE PUT UP AND TAKEN DOWN AT THE BEGINNING AND END OF EACH NAVIGATION SEASON, OWING TO THE PROBLEMS CAUSED BY ICE AND FLOODING. HOWEVER, GOODS WERE OFTEN UNLOADED ONTO THE QUAYS, THEN LOADED DIRECTLY ONTO ANOTHER BOAT, TRAIN OR CART— FOR DELIVERY TO THE WAREHOUSE-STORES ON COMMISSIONERS STREET OR ELSEWHERE IN THE CITY.

Working conditions improved after a long struggle

The longshoremen had to engage in some memorable strikes to earn better working conditions. The first union strikes took place early in the twentieth century—in 1903, 1907, 1911 . . .—but it was not until the 1966 work stoppage that a commission of enquiry was mandated to study those conditions.

Until 1960, the work was seasonal and there was no job security. Workers had to show up on the quays every morning and sometimes at noon to find out where they would actually be working. Nowadays job security is guaranteed, there is work all year long, and the workers phone in every evening between 6 p.m. and midnight to get the schedule and location of the next day's work. Wages have also gone up over the decades, rising from $.20 an hour in 1902 to $1.40 in 1950. In 2006, they were around $28 an hour. The time when the work did not require any special training is long past. Specific skills are now required.

The longshoremen's association, where it is said that knowledge is passed on from father to son, is subject to the Canada Labour Code, as the port area is under federal jurisdiction; hiring practices must therefore comply with regulations. As a result, 10% of the jobs are now reserved for women and 10% for visible minorities. Working alongside women on the quays must seem strange to many longshoremen of the old school, even though the union has for many years recognized equal rights and does not tolerate any discrimination based on race, gender or religion. The new workers must find it just as difficult to fit in as French Canadians did at the end of the nineteenth century, when the Irish community controlled the quays.

1877

1880   1881

WELL BEFORE THEY BECAME UNIONIZED, LONGSHOREMEN WENT ON STRIKE TO IMPROVE THEIR WORKING CONDITIONS. THE PORT AUTHORITIES WOULD THEN CALL IN THE MILITIA.

On the Lachine Canal, the first strikes took place as early as 1843. The workers went on strike again in 1878, when the Canal was being enlarged.

The first union strike in the port, known as the "Great Strike", took place in 1903. It lasted a month and was a stormy one: the companies hired strike breakers. At the time, the mayor assigned almost 2,500 militiamen to keep an eye on the port.

Chasing offenders: the police

Did you know that one of the oldest police services in Canada is found in the port of Montréal? The *Wharf Police* was created by an act of United Canada in 1851—compared with the Royal Canadian Mounted Police, which was not established until 1873. Before this, law and order was maintained on the water and on the quays by the officers of Trinity House of Quebec City. This organization was created in 1805 by the government of Lower Canada to ensure that navigation regulations were respected on the St. Lawrence and to look after the installation of lighthouses, beacons and buoys. It was also responsible for piloting, and for enacting and ensuring respect for regulations in order to put an end to the chaos that was a feature of every port. Its jurisdiction had been extended to include Montréal as of 1806.

In 1832, the Montréal office of the organization became independent: operating under the name of Trinity House of Montréal, it would thenceforth take on the management of the harbour—and therefore of the brand new Montréal Harbour Commission—with jurisdiction over navigation and piloting as far east as Quebec City.

The first police force, in 1851, was made up of twelve officers, under the direction of Major R. G. Johnson. In 1867, there were forty men, under the orders of Colonel St. Ormond. The area under their authority included the Lachine Canal, in addition to the waterfront.

Many changes took place in the years following. Between 1867 and 1889, official responsibility for the police was transferred from the Montréal Harbour Commission to the federal government. Then the federal government abolished the police force and handed port security over to the Montréal police. In 1913, however, the port police force was re-established. At the time, it consisted of a chief, three captains and eighty-five constables, whose task it was to patrol and protect an area extending from Windmill Point, at the mouth of the Canal, to the far end of the port, which kept expanding further east. The number of policemen varied from year to year and with the seasons: there were fewer policemen in the winter, when the port was closed to shipping.

The work required good physical condition and a solid build. In 1920, a newspaper article noted that the new policemen hired for the season were almost all former soldiers and that their heights ranged from 5 foot 9 to 6 foot 4. Their job was to direct traffic on the quays, where congestion was growing worse as the port developed, to keep the peace and protect ships, as well as to ensure that goods, which were often unloaded directly on the quays, were not stolen or allowed to deteriorate.

In the nineteenth century and at the beginning of the twentieth, the port was a relatively safe place, despite what some people said. Between 1913 and 1934, the number of arrests varied from 268 (1913) to 24 (1934), averaging about a hundred a year. When the First World War began in 1914, port security was increased, with armed officers posted at each entrance in the flood wall that enclosed the site: no entry without a pass! (These precautions are still in force in the port today.) This did not, however, stop the entry of smuggled goods. In 1915, 20 people were arrested for trafficking in opium—the confiscated drugs were handed over to the customs authorities.

The most common offense at the time? Horse-drawn vehicles breaking the speed limit! In the nineteenth century, trotting and galloping were prohibited on the quays: the only speed allowed was a "walk". Traffic was certainly heavy. In 1913, there were so many cart drivers on the quays and near the sheds and so many carriages waiting for steamship passengers that managing these comings and goings took most of the police force's energy. In 1923, the annual report mentions checking 18,000 carts and a similar number of taxi vehicles.

Deaths in the port were not registered systematically in the police force's annual reports, but in 1928, at least 38 were noted: 9 accidental deaths, 9 suicides, 3 sudden deaths and . . . 17 drownings, even though, as early as 1859, notices were posted along the quays prohibiting swimming in the port. Swimming in the river was permitted, but only in selected areas clearly demarcated by a fence. The water was polluted by industrial waste from the Lachine Canal, logs and city sewage. Epidemics swept through Montréal regularly, leading the authorities to enact measures to improve public health. When did this practice stop? That is another research subject for historians . . . but the answer is no doubt related to the city's construction of public swimming pools and the extension of water mains into homes.

PROVINCE OF CANADA,) BY THE MASTER. DEPUTY-MASTER AND WARDENS OF THE TRINITY
Port and Harbour of Montreal.) HOUSE OF MONTREAL, IN THE PROVINCE OF CANADA.

TO *Patrick Morgan*

Cab driver, or owner

Whereas complaint and information have been made before the Master, Deputy
Master and Wardens of the Trinity House of Montreal, by *Henry G.*
Thompson of the City of Montreal, in the District of Montreal, *H*
Water Bailiff that you did, *or a person employed by you,*
did, on Wednesday seventeenth instant, drive
Cab N° 89, along the wharf, at a fast
trot, between the hours of 12 o'clock and
1 P.M.;

contrary to the Rules and Regulations of the said Trinity House in such case
made and provided.

This is the text of the related summons, dated June 18, 1846, and attested by James Holmes, registrar of Trinity House of Montréal. The text does not say whether the speeding driver had to pay a fine, but according to Article 76 of the law, the sum in question could be as high as $40!

By the master, deputy-master and wardens of the Trinity House of Montréal, in the province of Canada

To Patrick Morgan, cabdriver or owner

Whereas complaint and information have been made before the Master, Deputy-Master and Wardens of the Trinity House of Montréal, by Henry G. Thompson of the City of Montréal, in the District of Montréal, Water Bailiff, that you did, or a person employed by you, did, on Wednesday seventeenth instant, drive Cab No 89, along the wharf, at a fast trot, between the hours of 12 o'clock and 1 P.M. contrary to the Rules and Regulations of the said Trinity House in such case made and provided.

IN 1928, THE PORT
POLICE FORCE HAD A
CHIEF, THREE CAPTAINS
AND SIXTY-THREE
CONSTABLES.

In a report in 1851, Major R. G. Johnson itemized police operations between August and December:

- 18 people saved from drowning
- 32 people sent to appear in front of the high courts
- 21 people arrested for theft
- 32 people arrested for assault and brawling
- 42 people arrested for drunkenness
- 15 deserters apprehended from the navy
- 3 people arrested for inciting sailors to desert
- 8 people arrested for disturbing workers
- 2 people arrested for having tried to cause a riot as Lord Elgin was boarding his ship

THE POLICE STATION
AS SEEN AROUND 1934
THROUGH THE TANGLE
OF OVERHEAD WIRES THAT
POWERED THE ELECTRIC
TRAINS. MAINTAINING
SECURITY ON THE QUAYS
BECAME MORE AND MORE
DIFFICULT WITH THE
INCREASE IN THE NUMBER
OF RAILWAY TRACKS
AND THE CONTINUOUS
COMINGS AND GOINGS OF
HORSE-DRAWN CARRIAGES,
WORKERS, FOOT TRAFFIC . . .
AND EVENTUALLY,
MOTOR-DRIVEN VEHICLES.

A port with a welcome for all

A GROUP OF SAILORS
AROUND 1880.

MONTREAL
SEAMEN'S CLUB
CLUB DE MARINS

A	B	H	Q	Z
(Alpha)	(Bravo)	(Hotel)	(Quebec)	(Zulu)

The International Code of Signals allows ships to communicate at a distance by hoisting one or more flags like these. Each represents a letter or a message, depending on what the ships want to communicate. The letters above represent messages that are still in common use—the others are now rarely used. The B, for example, means: "I am loading, unloading or carrying dangerous materials." It always flies by day on a loaded oil tanker. It is lowered at night so that the wind does not wear it out too quickly.

Sailors and their House

In 1862, a charitable organization, the Montréal Sailors' Institute, was established by Protestant businessmen and professionals involved in shipping activities to help sailors avoid the bad influences they might run up against in the port . . .

Material, social, moral and spiritual assistance was offered to meet the sailors' unique needs. At "Mariners' House", located on the corner of Commissioners Street and Place Royale—from 1875 to 1981—, sailors and officers had access to games, books, and newspapers, and were encouraged to attend meetings and religious services. The Institute also looked after sailors who died in Montréal: a burial plot was set aside for them in the Protestant cemetery on Mount Royal and their names were inscribed on the common tombstones.

In 1893, Catholics in Montréal founded the Catholic Sailors' Club, the first of its kind in the world. The club moved into a building the Grey Nuns had built in 1874, formerly occupied by the Hudson's Bay Company. This building, known as the Grey Nuns Stores II, still stands on the corner of De la Commune and St. Pierre streets.

Then, in 1968, the two organizations merged and became Mariners' House. Now located in shed 3 on Alexandra Quay, it still provides the same services—for example, books in several languages, including Bibles—regardless of race or religion.

THE FORMER CATHOLIC SAILORS' CLUB, ON THE CORNER OF DE LA COMMUNE AND ST. PIERRE STREETS.

LOCATED ON ALEXANDRA QUAY IS THE IBERVILLE PASSENGER TERMINAL SHED. ON THE SECOND FLOOR OF SHED 3, OPPOSITE THE MARINERS' HOUSE OFFICES, IS A ROW OF FLAGS REPRESENTING THE WORDS "PASSENGER TERMINAL" —IN FRENCH.

G A R E   M A R I T I M E

IN THE GAMES ROOM OF THE MONTRÉAL SAILORS' INSTITUTE (MARINERS' HOUSE), IN 1912.

THE ORIGINAL MONTRÉAL SAILORS' INSTITUTE BUILDING WAS REPLACED IN 1953 BY THIS BUILDING, WHICH THEN HOUSED THE "ŒUVRES DE LA MAISON DU PÈRE", WHERE MEN IN NEED COULD FIND SHELTER. TODAY IT BELONGS TO POINTE-À-CALLIÈRE, THE MONTRÉAL MUSEUM OF ARCHAEOLOGY AND HISTORY.

In 1860, workers on the Victoria Bridge put up a monument in memory of 6,000 British immigrants— mostly Irish from Griffintown—who died of typhus in 1846 and 1847.

In the first half of the nineteenth century, the Irish came to Canada in large numbers.

Large waves of immigrants

Between 1831 and 1861, the population of Montréal grew at the incredible rate of 58% per decade! Immigration was a major factor. In 1857, more than 32,000 immigrants travelling on 18 steamships and 217 sailing ships arrived in the port of Quebec City. English immigrants were in the majority (11,098), but there were also Norwegians (6,119), Scots (4,925), Germans (4,872), Irish (4,466), Swedes (351), Belgians (215) . . .

Many of these immigrants were heading for the area around the Great Lakes where some had jobs waiting for them; this was the case of the Woolwich Arsenal craftsmen, sent to Canada by the Wellington Fund Emigration Committee, after they had all been let go at the end of the Crimean War—the conflict between Imperial Russia and the Ottoman Empire on the shores of the Black Sea. But many others settled in Montréal, whose population, between 1851 and 1861, grew by an average of 3,260 people per year. The Irish population alone grew from 18,000 to 25,000 during this period. These immigrants, primarily English speaking, began to change the face of Mon-

tréal. However, a huge influx of rural families from Quebec, lured by the possibility of work in the new industries, gradually tipped the scales back in favour of Francophones.

In the early twentieth century, there was another sudden increase in the population of Montréal: from 216,650 inhabitants in 1891, the city grew to 467,986 by 1911 and then to 618,506 by 1921! The arrival of immigrants in the port played a major role in this growth. Although their nationalities were not recorded, there was a high proportion of Europeans, among them Italians, many of whom were working in the port in 1907. Russians, Ukrainians and Poles arrived as well—the majority were Jews fleeing the pogroms of the Russian czarist empire. There were also Chinese, coming from the Canadian West, where they had worked in railroad construction.

The new arrivals settled near the port at first—along St. Lawrence Boulevard where the new textile factories needed a large un-skilled work force. The Chinese settled just north of the old city, between Viger Street and Dorchester Boulevard (today René Lévesque

Boulevard); they opened laundries all over Montréal. The Jewish neighbourhood extended up St. Lawrence Boulevard as far as Mile End Station. Further to the north, the Boulevard would become the heart of Little Italy.

After the Second World War, St. Lawrence Boulevard received a new wave of immigrants, as large numbers of Greeks, Portuguese and Hungarians moved into areas that earlier waves had abandoned.

The most recent waves have continued to include people from Eastern Europe (Poles, Ukrainians, Romanians, etc.), but also from Asia, Africa, South-East Asia, the Caribbean and India. These families and their descendants are found today in Côte-des-Neiges, Parc-Extension and Saint-Michel. The 2001 census identified more than one hundred ethnic groups in the metropolitan region. They in turn are changing the face of the city, just as the Irish, Scots and French-Canadians did in the nineteenth century. A few desperate illegal immigrants also try to get into the country through the port, risking their lives by stowing away in containers.

Left
IN THE NINETEENTH CENTURY, IMMIGRANTS CROWDED ONTO SAILING SHIPS AND STEAMSHIPS. THESE SHIPS WERE KNOWN AS "COFFIN SHIPS", BECAUSE OF THE DREADFUL CONDITIONS ON BOARD.

Below
IN THE TWENTIETH CENTURY, AS A CONSEQUENCE OF MAJOR CONFLICTS, LARGE NUMBERS OF IMMIGRANTS ARRIVED IN MONTRÉAL.

A Scottish immigrant's journey

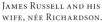
James Russell and his wife, née Richardson.

The port of Montréal, August 6, 1857. The Russell family—James, his wife Mary and their daughter Agnes—arrived on the steamship *SS Clyde* from Glasgow, Scotland.

James Russell kept a logbook. As a result, we know that the crossing took seventeen days and the family shared berths in steerage with one hundred and thirty-six other passengers, while 27 people had private cabins. During the voyage, they were served broth or pea soup, with fish and potatoes, beef or salt pork and biscuits during the week, and on Sundays roast beef, boiled beef and raisin pudding. The passengers had chores to do on the ship and had to keep their quarters clean.

Although seasickness affected some of the passengers, the crossing was quite pleasant and the sight of an iceberg off Newfoundland, rising about 70 feet above the water, delighted many. Tragedies like that of the Titanic had not yet made the headlines . . .

The compulsory medical examination, in the harbour at Quarantine Island, just east of Quebec City at Grosse-Île, went very well: the ship was allowed to continue on to Montréal. This was lucky, as at the time several thousand immigrants died during the crossings or at the quarantine stations at Grosse-Île, and near Montréal, at Point St. Charles.

No sooner had Russell arrived in Montréal than he was hired as a clerk by the Grand Trunk Railway Company. The Russells settled not in the St. Anne district, near the company's workshops in Point St. Charles, but rather in the St. Antoine district, near the Bonaventure Station (the former one) used by the trains of the Montréal and Lachine Company. Shortly after, the Russell family moved, first to St. Joseph Street, and then a little further north to St. Antoine Street. Quite soon, however, they moved further up toward the mountain, settling on Mountain Street, near Sherbrooke. They bought a piece of land on the newly subdivided Desrivières farm, next to the McTavish farm and the McGill lands. In the second half of the nineteenth century, this neighbourhood (now the city's downtown core) became home to the wealthiest citizens of Montréal, mainly Anglophones.

Meanwhile, Russell became a lumber agent, still working for the Grand Trunk. In 1880, according to the Lovell directory, he became a contractor. He left Montréal around 1883 for the Gaspé region, and settled in Ruisseau à Sem, near Méchins, where he held the cutting rights for lumber and saw-mills. He very likely used the contacts he had made while he worked for the Grand Trunk. Later on, he settled in Matane. James's last house, on the hillside, is still occupied by his descendants.

After the Russells' ship had stopped briefly in Quebec City and they had visited the town, a new captain took the helm to steer the sailing ship through the channel to Montréal. James Russell described his arrival in the big city this way:

"*We came into the quay of Montréal at 4 o'clock, fired off two cannons. Got all our luggage on shore. I got mine put into the shed till I got a place to put it into. Mary had been down looking for us yesterday and had been down two or three times today, but had to go back in the afternoon. James Brock and I went on shore after six o'clock and when we came back we saw Mary. She had spoken for a room for us and I went up and saw it and took it for a month till I got settled down. We all slept on board tonight again. Got up on Friday morning. Got my luggage to room and got things arranged pretty comfortably. The Brocks got advised by some men on shore, one they had never seen before, to go right up into the country, so they left Montréal on Friday morning at 9 o'clock for, I think, Kingston or Toronto. I was told today by a number of gentlemen that Montréal was in a better condition than either Kingston, Toronto, Hamilton or London, and was advised to settle down here in the meantime, which I have done.*"

LIKE MANY OTHER SCOTTISH-BORN MONTREALERS OF HIS GENERATION, JAMES RUSSELL WENT INTO BUSINESS. IN SO DOING, HE CONTRIBUTED, SOME YEARS LATER, TO THE DEVELOPMENT OF THE GASPÉ REGION.

1898

Innkeeper Joe Beef, in the nineteenth century, and restaurant owner Joseph Alfred Bousquet, in the twentieth, enshrined themselves forever in the hearts of Montrealers. As well, organizations aiming to keep up the sailors' morale or comfort those who were down on their luck opened their doors in the port or the surrounding area. Thus began a tradition of welcome and mutual assistance that continues today.

JOE BEEF HAD EVERYTHING IT TOOK TO BECOME A LEGEND: ANIMALS HE BOUGHT FROM SAILORS AND KEPT IN HIS CELLAR—BISON, BEARS, WOLVES, FOXES, WILD CATS . . . —, HIS OUTSPOKENNESS, HIS MIXED CLIENTELE AND, ABOVE ALL, A BIG HEART.

Joe Beef and his welcoming tavern

When Irishman Charles McKiernan arrived in Canada in 1861 (or in 1864?) with the 10th brigade of the Royal Regiment of Artillery, he found himself running the military canteen on St. Helen's Island. He was already known as Joe Beef, a nickname that came from his ability to find meat and other foodstuffs when he was a soldier in the Crimean War.

When he was released from the army, around 1868, McKiernan opened his first tavern on St. Claude Street, very near the new Market square (now Place Jacques Cartier) and Bonsecours Market, where most lodgings for travelers and port employees were located. Expropriated when the Gosford tunnel (now filled in) was constructed, he reopened in a building belonging to Pierre Beaudry, on the corner of De Callière and De la Commune streets.

Located a stone's throw from the port, Joe Beef's Canteen became a landmark institution. Its owner was more than just a colourful character with a menagerie to entertain his guests: he was a true philanthropist. He offered good meals to his better off customers, for example, steak and onions with bread, butter, tea and sugar for $.10, but he never refused a bowl of soup and a piece of bread to anyone who was unable to pay for it. He owned a farm at Longue-Pointe where he raised his own animals for slaughter, which meant he could prepare up to six hundred meals a day. His large income—earned from the sale of alcohol (beer, wine, cider and spirits)—allowed him to be as generous as he wanted.

The tavern was also an inn, with a hundred beds divided among ten rooms; its owner made sure his guests were clean by forcing those who needed it most to take a bath, even going so far as to sprinkle them with insecticide!

During the Lachine Canal strike in 1877, Joe Beef continued to earn the respect of the less fortunate by giving the strikers free soup and bread and allowing them to meet in his tavern. Three years later, he again stood with the workers by supporting the strikers at the Victor Hudon cotton-mill. Notre-Dame and Montréal General hospitals also benefited from his generosity, as did the Salvation Army (which took over the inn for a few years after his death in 1889). Nonetheless, selling alcohol drew the fire of temperance supporters, who called his inn a "den of iniquity".

Joe Beef was so beloved that at his funeral, one of the most imposing of the time, all those he had helped wanted to pay their respects, which forced offices in the business district to close down for the afternoon. Fifty labour organizations were represented. As for the famous tavern, the building was bought in 1903 and became the Star Café. Young leftists used it as a meeting place until it was closed in 1965. Yet the legend of Joe Beef lives on: a recently opened restaurant in Little Burgundy keeps alive the memory of the Irishman with the big heart.

JOE BEEF'S CANTEEN.

Nos 4, 5 & 6, Common Street MONTREAL.

Around 1885

Around 1910

Joe Beef's building in the twentieth century. When it was restored, all traces of the name disappeared.

1962

2006

The legend of Joe Beef lives on today in a restaurant bearing his name.

ALFRED BOUSQUET
SENIOR (1894-1947)

Joseph Alfred Bousquet and the Lunch

After Charles McKiernan, another chef, Joseph Alfred Bousquet, made a name for himself in the port. Around 1920, his father, Alfred, arrived with the family from Saint-Pie-de-Bagot: several children had died of the Spanish flu in 1918 and the family had decided to move to the city, as did many rural families at that time.

Immediately on arrival, Alfred Bousquet obtained a concession in the port of Montréal to sell his own spruce beer. In the years following, he was licensed to operate a restaurant and snack-bars in sheds 2 to 15. The whole family was involved in the business. In spite of this, Alfred soon returned to his farm. His oldest son, Joseph Alfred, took over as manager. He had long been interested in cooking and honed his skills working with his uncle, maître d'hotel at the Queen's, one of the best known hotels in Montréal at the time.

By then, the port was in the midst of rapid development. Nearly 5,000 people were working here! That meant a lot of mouths to feed … Of course, canteens had already been open on the quays for a long time. As early as 1858, given the uninterrupted flow of immigrants, the commissioners had granted several concessions. But in Joseph Alfred's time, all of the workers in the port had to eat here, as it was no longer possible to go back and forth freely between the city and the port: the long stone floodwall which extended from the Molson Brewery to the Mill Street Bridge, as well as the entrances into the port from the main streets, were guarded by the harbour police.

In 1936, the port was subdivided into eight sectors distributed among six restaurant owners: Passaretti, Ruffalo, Bousquet, Diamond, Roy and Ouellette. Each concession holder had snack-bars in the various sheds and buildings, as well as a main restaurant where hot meals were prepared. Joseph Alfred Bousquet had the monopoly of sectors three and four, which extended from the mouth of the Lachine Canal to Clock Tower Quay. His restaurant, the Lunch, was built against the flood wall near grain elevator 1, at the foot of Place Royale. Hot dishes were prepared on a wood stove. Cold meals were also prepared for the snack-bars in sheds 2 to 15, where travellers in transit, shipping company employees and sailors would stop to eat.

Joseph Alfred, an excellent cook, knew how to produce complicated meals complete with "pièces montées". The Lunch menu however was designed for a hard-working clientele. Full meals, from soup to dessert, and traditional dishes were on the menu: beef with vegetables, stews, meat pies. The restaurant was only open for breakfast and lunch. There was no alcohol served at the Lunch despite the fact that the Quebec government, unlike the rest of Canada, then in the middle of the Prohibition era, continued to authorize the sale of wine, beer and cider. A drink could only be had outside the walls of the port; it was best however not to forget your pass if you wanted to get back in!

During the Great Depression, the number of homeless people in the area around the port increased dramatically. Bousquet, taking his lead from Charles McKiernan, gave whatever surplus he had to the poor and soon had a regular following. Some, according to his daughter Lise, came to pay their respects at his funeral.

The homeless still receive food and help not far from where Bousquet was located. In 1894, after McKiernan's death, the Society of St-Vincent-de-Paul opened a soup kitchen, the "Fourneau économique". Rose-de-Lima Bonneau (1859-1934), a Grey Nun, took on the management of the shelter in 1904; after her death it was renamed the *Accueil Bonneau* or Bonneau shelter. The current building is not the original; it was rebuilt in 1998 in an almost identical style, following a major fire caused by a gas explosion. Its staff carry on the humanitarian work of the port's former chefs.

JOSEPH ALFRED
BOUSQUET DEVELOPED
HIS PASSION FOR
COOKING THANKS TO
THE GUIDANCE OF HIS
UNCLE, MAITRE D'HOTEL
AT THE QUEEN'S.
THE LUNCH WAS
A FAMILY BUSINESS,
WHERE IRÈNE BOUSQUET
AND THE CHILDREN
ALL LENT A HAND.

IT IS STILL POSSIBLE TO HAVE
A MEAL IN THE OLD PORT,
WHETHER ON A PATIO OR
PICNIC-STYLE. NEARBY,
OLD MONTRÉAL ALSO HAS
RESTAURANTS AND HOTELS
TO SATISFY EVERY TASTE.

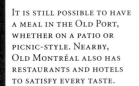

The hosts of today

No longer do longshoremen, track layers or grain elevator operators come to work in the Old Port of Montréal every morning. Nowadays people with a very wide range of backgrounds, training and jobs are working to make the new vision for the site a reality: to create a great city and maritime park, where people can reconnect with the port's history and with its technological and festive heritage, and thus be a part of the activity taking place here today.

Among those who work in the Old Port occasionally or full-time, there are of course the regular and seasonal employees of the Corporation; as many as 360 employees may work here in the high summer season, when many students are hired on a temporary basis. Many other people also work here, however, for businesses or organizations: cruise company operators, exhibition and event designers, landscape architects, concession holders, restaurant owners, artists and craftspeople, environmentalists and promoters from the worlds of entertainment, theatre, arts and literature . . .

These individuals all develop a connection with the site that either directly or indirectly enhances the welcome given to visitors. A programming officer works with a Montréal cultural community to produce a new festival. A lock operator carries on the work of the past using present-day equipment, while explaining to her curious visitors the workings of these technical structures, rarely seen in an urban setting. A gallery attendant from the Montréal Science Centre tries to find a way to help children understand a scientific phenomenon. The IMAX projectionist lets a multimedia artist or a producer use the screening room to check film takes. A logistics specialist sees to it that the needs of the Cirque du Soleil are met so the big top can be set up . . . just a few of the behind the scenes activities rooted in the spirit of innovation underlying the development of the port.

An Old Port to make your own

Gone are the days when you had to show a pass to enter the old section of the port. The Old Port, now open 365 days a year, offers Montrealers and tourists a range of activities that seek to make the most of all the attributes—not all of them recent—of a site where land and water, city and river, meet.

THE AMPHI-BUS HAS DRIVEN OFF DE LA COMMUNE STREET AND INTO THE WATER.

. . . on foot, on skates, by bicycle, by boat

Today, most people visit the Old Port of Montréal on foot, all year round. However, there are many other ways to get around the site. In the summer, you can put on a pair of in-line skates, hop on a bicycle, share a quadricycle, or ride on a *Segway*, a type of small electric scooter. Visitors will find traditional calèches in De la Commune Street. You can tour around on a pedal-boat, board an amphibious vehicle or take advantage of the shuttles or cruise boats.

And in winter? Now that there is less snow and cold spells are less frequent, it has become more difficult to go on sleigh rides, don cross-country skis and take in ice sculpture competitions than in the 1990s. But nothing stops you from lacing up your skates and heading for Bonsecours Basin, where you can glide past the remains of the pier where grain elevator 2 once stood and around the foundations of the former conveyor galleries—to the sound of a group playing traditional music on certain days in December. Or you can take in a techno concert in the middle of January on a big outdoor stage on Jacques Cartier Quay.

Centre
GETTING AROUND ON A "SEGWAY".

Left
A PEDAL-BOAT CUTS ACROSS BONSECOURS BASIN AS THE SUN SETS OVER THE CITY.

All summer, the Old Port is full of tourists and workers from Old Montréal looking for some greenery and open spaces. Non-motorized pleasure vehicles are another attraction for those who don't mind using their legs.

Some of the Old Port motor-driven vehicles, reflecting environmental concerns, run on electricity or biodiesel, as was the case with the Biomer pilot project, developed jointly with the cruise companies in 2004.

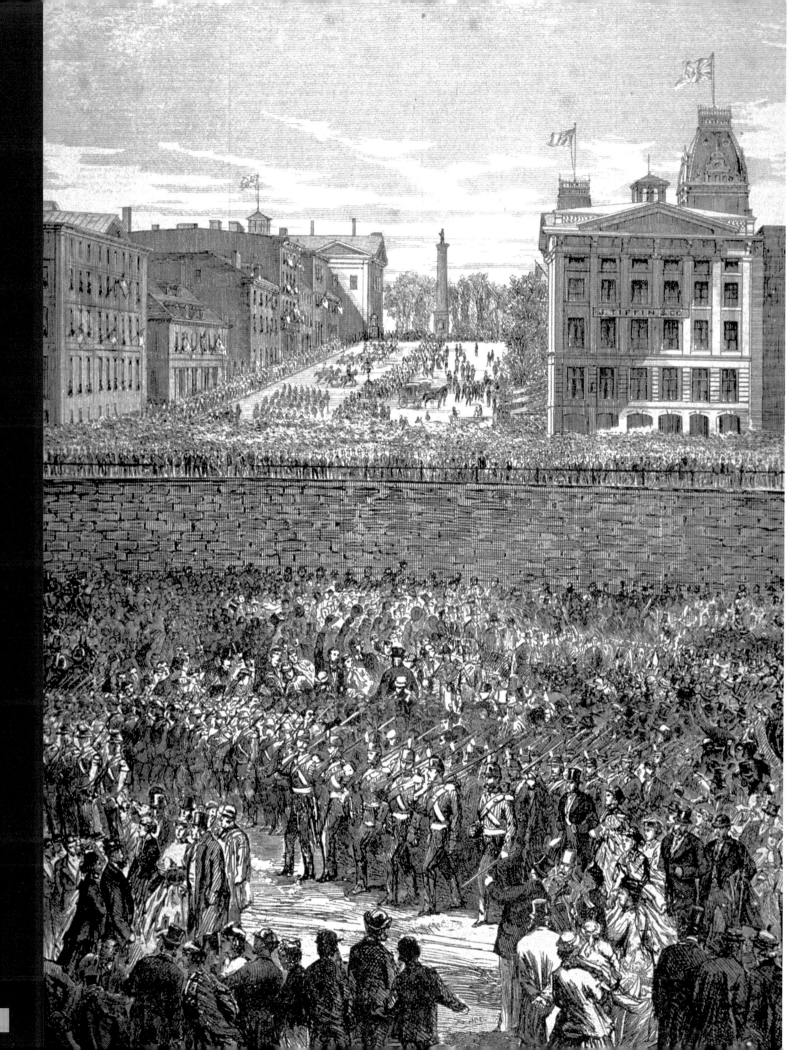

The goal in restoring the Old Port was to give back to Montrealers the access to the river that had been taken away when the flood wall was built and when access was prohibited after 1914. This link has been re-established not by import-export activities, but through recreation, tourism and festivities—just like the large gatherings of the past. On the left, celebrating the Queen's birthday in 1879. On the right, a lively spot: where Place Jacques Cartier meets the quay of the same name.

2006

1880

FESTIVE EVENTS HAVE
ALWAYS ATTRACTED
CROWDS TO THE SITE.
BELOW, PEOPLE
BOARDING STEAMSHIPS
TO CELEBRATE THE
QUEEN'S BIRTHDAY, THIS
TIME IN QUEBEC CITY.
ABOVE, IN 2006, THE
CROWD SQUEEZING ONTO
THE PROMENADE
ALONGSIDE BONSECOURS
BASIN ON CANADA DAY.

Then: Fireworks mark the inauguration of Victoria Bridge.

Now: Telus Fire on Ice splashes its colours over the Old Port skating rink.

1860

2005

1855

The joys of winter:
curling, ice lacrosse, velocipede riding, bicycles . . .

The site has a long tradition of winter sports. In the nineteenth century, while shipping was closed down from November to April, labourers as well as ladies and gentlemen of high society liked to come down to the port to enjoy their favourite activity.

19th century

DURING THE QUEBEC WINTER
CARNIVAL, CROSSING THE RIVER
BY CANOE IS AN EXPERIENCE
NOT TO BE MISSED. BUT AS THIS
ENGRAVING SHOWS, THIS
TRADITIONAL SPORT WAS ALSO
PRACTISED IN THE PORT OF
MONTRÉAL IN THE WINTER.

ADVENTUROUS FANS
OF HIGH-WHEEL
BICYCLES HAVING FUN.
IN THE BACKGROUND,
CALÈCHES USED THE
ICE BRIDGE THAT
CONNECTED THE
BANKS OF THE RIVER
AT THE TIME.

A SKATING RINK WAS
BUILT NEAR THE ROYAL
INSURANCE BUILDING.

1870

AROUND 1860,
JOHN HENRY WALKER
(1831-1899) SKETCHED
THIS WINTER SCENE
SOMEWHERE BETWEEN
PLACE JACQUES CARTIER
AND BONSECOURS
MARKET. THE STONE
WALL RUNNING ALONG
COMMISSIONERS STREET
CAN BE SEEN CLEARLY. ON
THE RIGHT, A GAME OF ICE
LACROSSE IS UNDERWAY.

BONSECOURS BASIN HAS
UNDERGONE MANY
CHANGES SINCE THE 1840S.
FOR MANY YEARS, IT
WELCOMED BOATS LOADED
WITH HAY, FRUIT AND
VEGETABLES TO BE SOLD IN
THE MARKET OPPOSITE AND
IN PLACE JACQUES
CARTIER. IT WAS
COMPLETELY REDEVELOPED
AT THE BEGINNING OF THE
TWENTIETH CENTURY AND
FILLED IN AROUND 1970 SO
A CONTAINER TERMINAL
COULD BE BUILT. FINALLY,
THE OLD PORT OF
MONTRÉAL CLEARED IT
OUT TO CREATE A SPACE
WHERE PEOPLE COULD
ENJOY ACTIVITIES ON THE
WATER IN THE SUMMER AND
ON THE ICE IN THE WINTER.
THE SKATING RINK IN THE
OLD PORT NOW HAS AN
ARTIFICIAL SECTION,
EXTENDED, AS SOON AS THE
WEATHER IS COLD ENOUGH,
BY A NATURAL ICE OVAL.

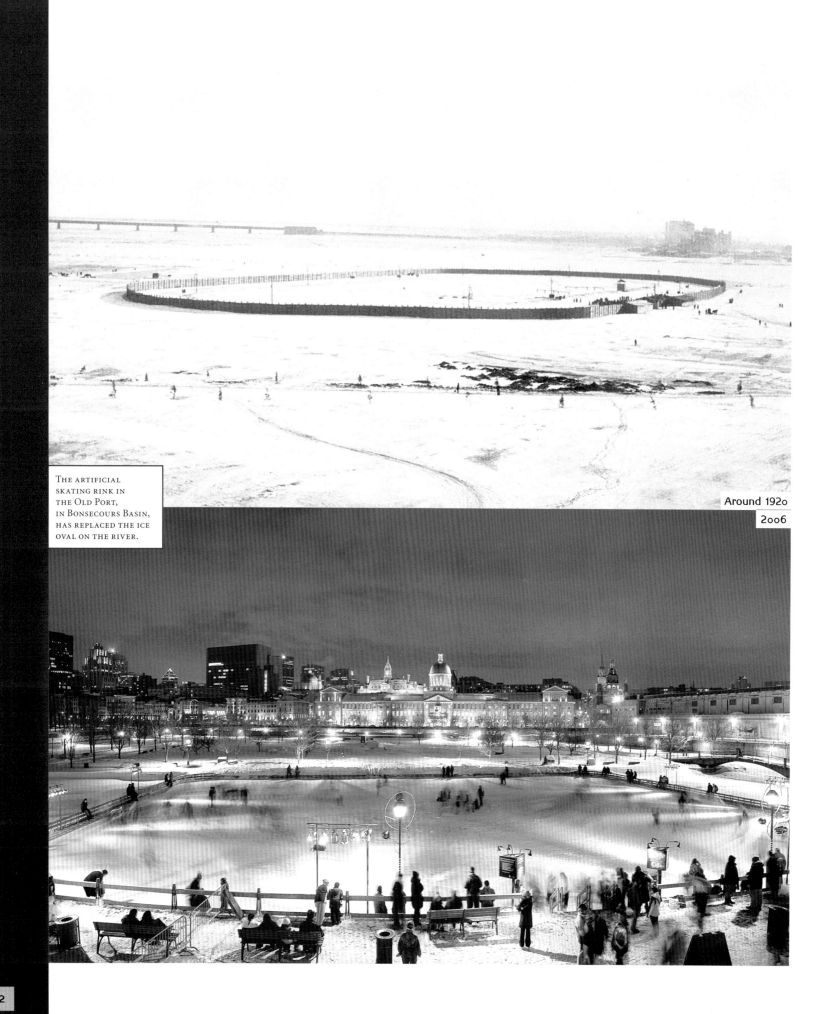

THE ARTIFICIAL SKATING RINK IN THE OLD PORT, IN BONSECOURS BASIN, HAS REPLACED THE ICE OVAL ON THE RIVER.

Around 1920

2006

2006

1881

GETTING READY FOR
THE ICE CUP, A
FRIENDLY RACE
BETWEEN THE BEST
BICYCLE COURIERS FROM
CANADA AND THE
UNITED STATES. DO
THESE DARING CYCLISTS
KNOW THAT BETWEEN
1868 AND 1871
VELOCIPEDE RACES
WERE VERY POPULAR, AS
WERE SKATING RACES?
THE HIGH-WHEEL
BICYCLE WAS ECLIPSED
BY THE REGULAR
BICYCLE AROUND 1880.

THE BEST SNOWBOARDERS
FROM QUEBEC AND CANADA
COMPETED AGAINST EACH
OTHER IN THE OLD PORT IN
FEBRUARY 2006 IN A RAMP
SNOWBOARDING
COMPETITION, THE BIGGEST
OF ITS KIND EVER HELD IN
ANY CANADIAN CITY.

. . . sliding, snowboarding!

IN 2006, THE SLIDE IN
PLACE JACQUES CARTIER,
INSTALLED FOR THE
MONTRÉAL HIGH LIGHTS
FESTIVAL, WAS AS
POPULAR AS THE ONE SET
UP IN 1887. AT THE TIME,
SLIDING WAS PART OF THE
MONTRÉAL CARNIVAL, A
POPULAR CELEBRATION
ORGANIZED BY THE
MONTRÉAL SNOWSHOE
CLUB THAT WAS HELD

FIVE TIMES IN DIFFERENT
PARTS OF THE CITY
BETWEEN 1883 AND 1889.
THE THEN ARCHBISHOP
OF MONTRÉAL, MGR.
ÉDOUARD-CHARLES
FABRE, WARNED HIS
CATHOLIC FLOCK THAT
THIS ACTIVITY, ENJOYED
BY MEN AND WOMEN
TOGETHER, WAS IN HIS
VIEW "A PROBABLE
OCCASION FOR SIN".

AN ICE SCULPTURE BY
ARTIST LAURENT GODON
FOR *FANTASY ON ICE*.

THE OLD PORT ILLUMINATED
DURING THE MONTRÉAL
HIGH LIGHTS FESTIVAL IN 2006.

IN THE DEAD OF WINTER,
SHIPS DOCKED IN THE OLD
PORT COMBINE THEIR
POWERFUL VOICES TO
PERFORM A MOST UNUSUAL
MUSICAL COMPOSITION, IN
AN URBAN CONCERT THAT IS
AS PLAYFUL AS IT IS LOUD:
THE PORT SYMPHONIES OF
POINTE-À-CALLIÈRE.

THE FIRST LIVE OUTDOOR
NATIVITY SCENE IN
MONTRÉAL WAS SET UP IN
THE OLD PORT IN DECEMBER
1992. VERY POPULAR WITH
THE PUBLIC, IT WAS
RECREATED SEVERAL TIMES.

The pleasures of summer: events, festivals, performances . . .

The Old Port of Montréal Corporation learned early on to manage large-scale events. Both one-of-a-kind and repeated events usually take place on Jacques Cartier Quay: Canada Day, rock concerts, Cirque du Soleil premieres, the Montréal Beer Festival, where visitors are encouraged to sample a drink enjoyed in so many countries, the Just for Laughs Festival, the Montréal High Lights Festival, some of the events of Italian Week, the *I Read Montréal* exhibit, part of the "Montréal, World Book Capital" year, the Montréal International Reggae Festival, the Festival International Expo Art Montréal, welcoming more than 500 renowned and up and coming artists in painting, drawing, sculpture, photography and calligraphy, among many others.

Centre
IN JULY 2006, ON CANADA DAY, THE SKI JUMPERS OF THE "QUEBEC AIR FORCE" PUT ON SPECTACULAR DEMONSTRATIONS.

Below
IN 1988, ON KING EDWARD QUAY, *THE DRAGONS TRILOGY* BY ROBERT LEPAGE WAS PRODUCED IN SHED 9, RIGHT AFTER THE PLAY'S ACCLAIMED PERFORMANCE AT THE FESTIVAL DE THÉÂTRE DES AMÉRIQUES.

CIRQUE DU SOLEIL STAGES
ITS WORLD PREMIERE
PERFORMANCES FOR
MONTREALERS ON
JACQUES CARTIER QUAY.

SINCE 2004, THE SITE HAS
WELCOMED EXCELLENT
MUSICIANS AND
STORYTELLERS FOR THE
MONTRÉAL INTERNATIONAL
REGGAE FESTIVAL. THIS
EVENT, WITH SPECIAL TIES TO
THE JAMAICAN COMMUNITY,
IS THE MAIN FESTIVAL OF ITS
KIND IN NORTH AMERICA.

IN 1991, A FRENCHWOMAN WHO
LOVED BOOKS, HÉLÈNE TIROL, SAW
IN THE QUAYS OF THE OLD PORT
AN IDEAL SPOT FOR MONTREALERS
TO TASTE THE PLEASURES OF
BROWSING THROUGH SECOND-
HAND BOOKSTALLS SO FAMILIAR
TO PARISIANS ON THE BANKS OF
THE SEINE. THUS WAS BORN ONE
OF THE FIRST GROUPS TO PLAY
A ROLE IN REVITALIZING
THE PORT: LES BOUQUINISTES
DU SAINT-LAURENT. THE
BOOKSELLERS' STALLS ARE OPEN
FOR A MONTH IN THE SUMMER.
MUSICAL PERFORMANCES,
FILMS AND CONFERENCES
ALL ENCOURAGE READING.

. . . and romance

ON THE RIGHT, BOATMAN JOS VINCENT, DRESSED TO THE NINES, WAITED, PADDLE IN HAND, TO RENT HIS CANOES. NOWADAYS, LOVERS FLOAT AROUND IN PEDAL-BOATS ON BONSECOURS BASIN. MINIATURE BOATS (LEFT) CAN ALSO BE RENTED.

1875

EVERY SUNDAY IN SUMMER, COUPLES GET SWEPT UP IN A SALSA FRENZY THAT TAKES PLACE AT THE END OF KING EDWARD QUAY, SURROUNDED IN MUSIC FOR THE OCCASION.

In the nineteenth century, the top of the stone wall was also the sidewalk on Commissioners Street. People could walk along it and look out onto the port. Today it is possible to stroll everywhere in the Old Port, whether along the second-floor gallery of the Jacques Cartier Pavilion or around the edges of the large quays. Boats and dress may have changed, but love . . .

1878

1870

2006

Then and now

WHERE ONCE THE WOOD
USED TO FUEL THE STEAM
ENGINES WAS PILED HIGH ON
THE QUAYS, TREES HAVE BEEN
PLANTED: A BICYCLE PATH
NOW RUNS ALONG DE LA
COMMUNE STREET, WIDER
NOW THAN WHEN IT WAS
KNOWN AS COMMISSIONERS
STREET. FOLLOW THE CYCLIST
ON THE RIGHT TO THE
WESTERNMOST END OF THE
OLD PORT, INTO THE LOCK
GARDENS—NOT WITHOUT
NOTING IN PASSING THE
PORTION OF THE FLOODWALL
THAT CAN STILL BE SEEN
BETWEEN THE PATH AND
THE STREET.

Plant sculptures

In the summer of 2000, on the strip of land that was redeveloped in 1992 between locks 1 and 2—then called the Lock Park—, Montrealers were treated to an exhibition of plant art and sculpture displaying the best of horticultural know-how. This first international competition, on the theme "the planet is a mosaic" and organized by Mosaicultures International of Montréal in collaboration with the city of Montréal, was acclaimed by the public and immediately adopted by big cities worldwide. Two more similar exhibitions were held on the site.

In the Lock Gardens

Imaginative displays

In 2006, the International Flora Montréal put landscape art on display near the locks. This time, the aim was to show the public the designs of artists working with plants and space and to help further interest and training in horticulture and landscaping. The event is being repeated in 2007.

ANOTHER VIEW OF
MONTRÉAL, FROM
SOUTH BASIN 1 AND THE
LOCK GARDENS DURING
THE INTERNATIONAL
FLORA MONTRÉAL.

Nine editions of Expotec

In centuries past, the port of Montréal was the birthplace of many technical innovations. Today, the Montréal Science Centre carries on this tradition by informing the public about Canadian innovations while seeking to give young people a taste for science.

A number of events led to its creation. In the summer of 1987, the Engineering Centennial Board marked the one hundredth anniversary of the profession in Canada by inaugurating an exhibition, in sheds 7 and 9 on King Edward Quay, on the great feats of Canadian engineering. "Expotec 87" attracted more than 255,000 visitors. It would be the first of nine exhibitions—on health, communications, music, chemistry . . . To explore the links between science, technology and society, the exhibitions used only interactive displays and depended on educators to interest young people as well as adults, through demonstrations and participatory theatre.

At the same time, in shed 8 next door, the Canadian Museum of Science and Technology presented an exhibition on holography, which was also popular. Later, along with repeat versions of Expotec, a series of summer exhibitions, produced by the Cité des arts et des nouvelles technologies and entitled "Images of the future", gave Montrealers a glimpse of new horizons in the world of 2D and 3D images.

In 1988, another event took place: in shed 9, Montrealers experienced the first IMAX movie theatre in Quebec. This innovation was developed for Expo 67 in Montréal and the current IMAX technology was created for the Osaka World's Fair in Japan in 1970—it was then fine-tuned in Toronto.

Montrealers and tourists quickly adopted these spaces, where they were encouraged to handle the exhibits and have fun while learning. During the first five years, the Expotec/IMAX combination attracted more than 3 million visitors, 390,000 in the summer of 1995 alone. The groundwork was laid for the museum of science and technology that Quebec had been dreaming of for twenty years.

1989

COMING UP—EXPOTEC AND
IMAGES OF THE FUTURE

Not so long ago, on King Edward Quay

Long housed in shed 8, the Flea Market sold rare and unusual objects among the charming bric-a-brac in its hundred or so stalls. In the 1990s, it was the best known flea market in Montréal. Its neighbour at the time, *SOS Labyrinthe,* a game for groups to play in a huge canvas labyrinth, is now located on Clock Tower Quay, under the name *Le Labyrinthe du Hangar 16.*

The Old Port IMAX theatre

The IMAX®TELUS
AMPHITHEATRE IN THE
MONTRÉAL SCIENCE CENTRE.

In Canada, Montrealers were among the first to discover IMAX. They were soon won over. Using a cinematographic film of large dimensions and a screen seven storeys tall, the picture is so precise and the visual field so full that the spectator actually feels the camera movements: high angle shots, swooping like a bird . . . Added to these sensations are special effects and never before seen perspectives on nature, all of which make it an educational and enjoyable experience.

Nearly twenty years after its opening, the IMAX®TELUS theatre of the Montréal Science Centre, as it is now known, remains among the ten most popular of its kind. It shows movies that take maximum advantage of the technology and showcase the beauty of nature, unexplored lands, extreme experiences. It lets the spectator get closer than ever to the world of plants and animals, in the company of explorers and scientists. The theatre itself has continued to improve. In January 2006, the Old Port installed a Kanga sound system, the best in the world, with six speakers having a combined power of more than 36,000 watts. It is also one of only three theatres that can show IMAX films in high-definition.

Since the film *Imagine* (1994), the Old Port Corporation has regularly collaborated in film production and post-production and has often produced the French versions. Note that *The Old Man and the Sea*, produced by the Montréal company Productions Pascal Blais, was the first large format film to win an Oscar.

THE IMAX PROJECTION ROOM

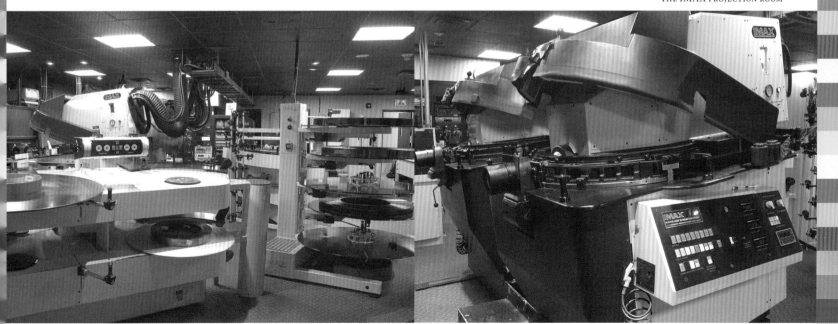

The Montréal Science Centre

In 1995, following the success of the Expotec exhibitions and with the aim of giving the city a permanent centre for science and technology, the Old Port of Montréal Corporation added to its development plan the restoration of King Edward Quay and its four sheds, to house a multifunctional complex. In addition to federal government support, the project received that of numerous businesses, all with the same goals: to make the public more aware of science and technology, to encourage young people to take an interest in scientific and technical careers, to raise the profile of home-grown innovations, to assist in training teachers and to participate in developing Montréal's economy and tourism sector.

Since it opened on May 1, 2000, the Centre has welcomed more than a million visitors—primary and secondary school students, families and adults of all ages. Among its many programs, one initiative deserves special mention as a first in North America: the opening in 2004, in cooperation with the Université du Québec à Montréal, of the in vivo laboratory for university education, a continuing education training centre for teachers and students learning to teach science and technology.

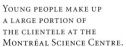

YOUNG PEOPLE MAKE UP
A LARGE PORTION OF
THE CLIENTELE AT THE
MONTRÉAL SCIENCE CENTRE.

Among the activities offered at the Montréal Science Centre have been the popular *Robofollies* during spring break and temporary exhibitions like *X-treme Rotation* and *Autopsy of a Murder*, winners of several prizes.

T he Old Port today is of course unique in also offering

water sports, another link between the port's past

and present. Many phantom boats haunt the quays . . .

A river teeming with life

The waters of the Old Port of Montréal used to host nearly every type of ship—and, even today, the port is still a maritime meeting place. Yachts and small sailboats bob up and down in the marina. The quays invite you to board a shuttle and spend some time on the islands, enjoy an evening meal while watching the sun set over the city, or take a turbulent ride through the rapids. Passenger ships with their tall white hulls dock at the Iberville Passenger Terminal just long enough for the cruise passengers to breathe in the welcoming air of Montréal. Sometimes you can even see lakers, long motorized barges designed for sailing conditions on and between the Great Lakes, as well as a number of cargo ships waiting to proceed to their destination. And that's not counting the apprentice sailing ships, ships of the Canadian Navy and the replicas of ships of days gone by that are open to visitors. Welcome to Montréal, now, as always, a beautiful and vibrant seaport . . .

PRECEDING PAGES
THE MARINA AT
JACQUES CARTIER BASIN.

LEFT
LAKERS ARE TEMPORARILY
DOCKED ON BOTH SIDES
OF CONVEYOR QUAY.

A parade of ships

IN THE SECOND HALF OF
THE NINETEENTH CENTURY,
SEVERAL OCEAN-GOING
THREE-MASTERS WERE
EQUIPPED WITH STEAM
ENGINES. SUCH WAS THE
CASE WITH THE *HMS
TOURMALINE*, A MASTED
CORVETTE OF THE
EMERALD CLASS OF THE
BRITISH ROYAL NAVY,
SHOWN HERE IN 1879
DOCKED AT THE MILITARY
QUAY, SLIGHTLY TO THE
EAST OF THE FORMER
VICTORIA PIER.

Montréal's harbour has always been a transit spot for people and goods and therefore a place where sea and land transport converge—an "intermodal" site. But the boats have changed enormously over the centuries, in design as well as in size, materials and means of propulsion. In fact, nearly the whole of navigation history has sailed past the city.

THE DUGOUT CANOE—A
CRAFT PATIENTLY CARVED
OUT OF A TREE TRUNK—
WAS USED BY NATIVE
PEOPLES, AS WELL AS BY
EUROPEANS, UNTIL AS
LATE AS THE NINETEENTH
CENTURY. THIS EXAMPLE
IS PRESERVED IN THE
CHATEAU RAMEZAY
MUSEUM IN MONTRÉAL.

THIS PRINT BY JOHN
RICHARD COKE SMYTH
CLEARLY SHOWS THE RANGE
OF WATERCRAFT ARRIVING
IN THE PORT OF MONTRÉAL
IN 1843.

CARGO SHIPS WINTER
TODAY IN THE OLD PORT,
WEIGHING ANCHOR WHEN
THE FINE WEATHER
ARRIVES.

Before the canals were constructed: with oar and sail

In the sixteenth and seventeenth centuries, when the first European ships carrying cod fishermen, whale hunters and explorers crossed the Atlantic and sailed into the Gulf of St. Lawrence, the ships were basically powered by sails and oars. The deeper the draught, the more dangerous it was for the boat to advance. A birchbark canoe or a dugout could glide safely over sandbanks or make it easily through rapids—with the option of portaging when rowing upstream was impossible even for the strongest men. A large sailing vessel on the other hand . . .

As a result, in order to navigate between Montréal, Kingston and the Great Lakes, travellers, coureurs des bois and hired hands used various canoes, one of which was the *Montréal canoe,* also called the *master's canoe.* These vessels were designed to carry tools, weapons, kegs of spirits and other goods to be exchanged at trading posts and to bring back furs that would be shipped to Europe. They could hold, depending on their size, from four to ten men.

At the end of the eighteenth century, military canoes were adapted to make it easier to transport men and ammunition over whitewater: the rapids of Coteau-du-Lac, Rocher-Fendu, Faucille and Trou-du-Moulin. The first craft used for this purpose resembled modified canoes, with pointed ends, a flat bottom and an auxiliary sail, and were known as *batteaux*—with two t's—in both French and English. Each could carry up to four and a half tonnes of goods and had a draught of only sixty centimetres.

Another flat-bottomed craft, American in origin, appeared at the beginning of the nineteenth century: the *Durham Boat.* Much larger than a batteau, they could carry up to forty tonnes of goods. They were so large that the military canals of Coteau-du-Lac and Rocher-Fendu had to be widened and deepened and those of Trou-du-Moulin and de la Faucille had to be replaced by the Cascades Canal. When the Lachine Canal was dug, between 1821 and 1825, it was ascertained that the locks were large enough to hold the biggest Durham Boat. *Barges* were also used.

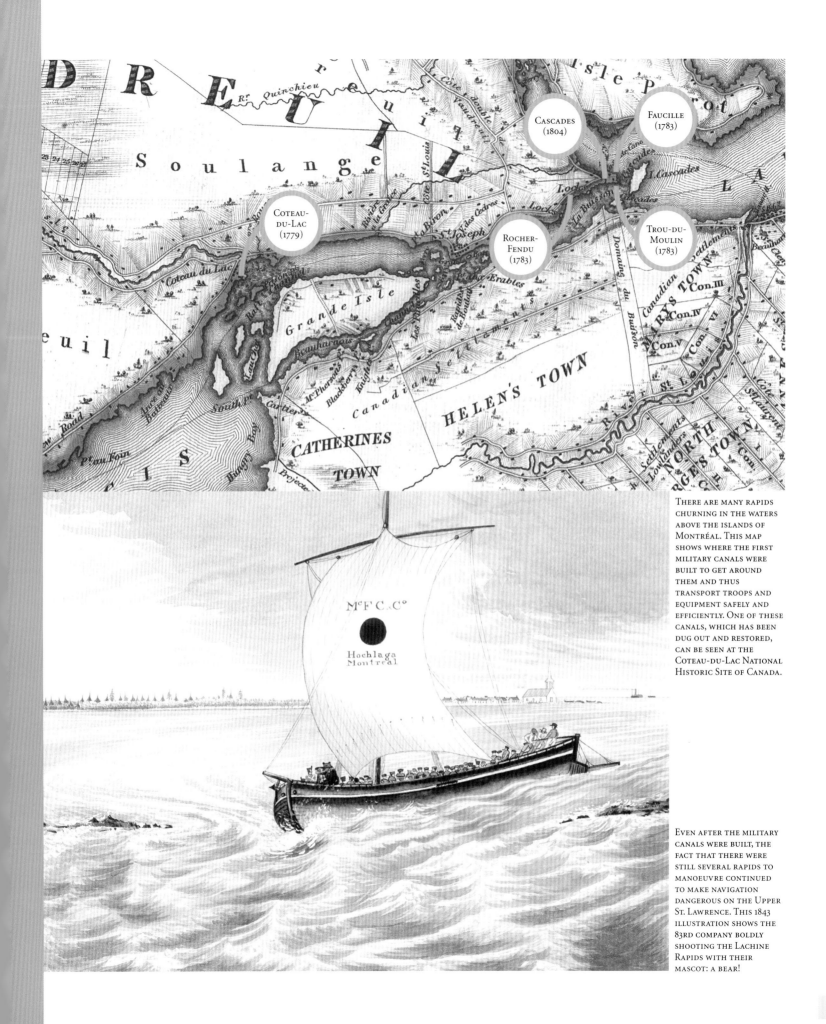

CASCADES
(1804)

FAUCILLE
(1783)

COTEAU-DU-LAC
(1779)

ROCHER-FENDU
(1783)

TROU-DU-MOULIN
(1783)

McF C &Cº

Hochlaga
Montreal

THERE ARE MANY RAPIDS CHURNING IN THE WATERS ABOVE THE ISLANDS OF MONTRÉAL. THIS MAP SHOWS WHERE THE FIRST MILITARY CANALS WERE BUILT TO GET AROUND THEM AND THUS TRANSPORT TROOPS AND EQUIPMENT SAFELY AND EFFICIENTLY. ONE OF THESE CANALS, WHICH HAS BEEN DUG OUT AND RESTORED, CAN BE SEEN AT THE COTEAU-DU-LAC NATIONAL HISTORIC SITE OF CANADA.

EVEN AFTER THE MILITARY CANALS WERE BUILT, THE FACT THAT THERE WERE STILL SEVERAL RAPIDS TO MANOEUVRE CONTINUED TO MAKE NAVIGATION DANGEROUS ON THE UPPER ST. LAWRENCE. THIS 1843 ILLUSTRATION SHOWS THE 83RD COMPANY BOLDLY SHOOTING THE LACHINE RAPIDS WITH THEIR MASCOT: A BEAR!

Transporting timber: the "cage"

At the turn of the nineteenth century, timber gradually replaced fur as the main product being shipped through the port of Montréal. An ingenious system was developed to transport the timber downstream from the Ottawa River valley and the Great Lakes: pieces of wood were assembled to make a raft that was sturdy enough to manoeuvre easily through the rapids and past the rocks and other obstacles along the Upper St. Lawrence. It was important that the fastenings not damage the pieces of wood, which, at the end of their journey, would be taken apart and sold as construction wood.

The base of the raft or cage, called a crib, was made of two frames of wood, measuring 18 by 12.5 metres, underneath which two logs were attached crosswise to act as floats and inside which the logs were laid. No screws or nails were used so as not to leave holes in the wood. Once four or five cribs were ready, they were tied together, forming a timber dram on which tents were then set up, as well as a cookhouse where meals for a team of about thirty men, known as raftsmen, could be prepared. Sails made the trip downriver easier. Later, steam-powered tugboats pulled the rafts.

Once the cage arrived in Montréal, the next step was to join 12 to 16 of these rafts in a row to make a log boom that would then continue on to Quebec City. There the timber would be shipped to construction sites, or, more often, loaded onto ocean-going ships heading for England.

Before the quays were built in the port of Montréal, the raftsmen landed directly on the shore in front of Bonsecours Market, just beyond the Sault Normand Rapids and before St. Mary's current. After 1825, they used the brand new Lachine Canal to bypass the rapids—and understandably so! However, in the end, the authorities prohibited them from using the Canal because the heavy rafts caused too much damage to the banks of the canal and the walls of the locks. In any event, at the end of the nineteenth century, thanks to improvements in the canal system, barges were able to replace for good the cages used for transporting timber from the West. Similarly, the dredging of the St. Lawrence channel allowed ocean liners to load wood right in Montréal, marking the end of the long log booms heading for Quebec City. However, this technique for transporting timber through the rough waters of the Upper St. Lawrence and the Ottawa River lives on in an extreme sport: rafting!

Several boats can be seen in this watercolour by Robert Auchmuty Sproule, painted around 1830: a paddle steamer, a square-rigged boat, a single-masted sailboat—and a raft with sails.

WINDMILL POINT, ON THE ST. LAWRENCE RIVER.

Cages arrive in the port of Montréal after making it through the Lachine Rapids, passing under the Victoria Bridge and circumventing Windmill Point.

In 1830, also sketched by Robert Auchmuty Sproule, a three-master, a paddle-steamer and a birchbark canoe meet at the mouth of the Little St. Pierre River. The construction of the quays had just begun, but the small island on which the first one would be built was already being used for storage.

*In the days of the sailing ship, sailing
upstream was . . . difficult: opposing
currents, unfavourable winds, a narrow channel making it hard to tack into the wind, the
presence of shoals and sandbars, etc. Going
downstream was easier, as sailors were
helped by the current and by the prevailing
winds from the west that filled the sails.*

GILLES ROUSSEAU,
geographer and sailor, 2007
[free translation]

Hoist the main sail!

The great sailing ships had long been a
common sight in the port of Montréal.
Even at the beginning of the twentieth century they were still seen, mainly used for cabotage—sailing at a short distance from the
banks—on the St. Lawrence.

From 1760 to 1850, various kinds of sailing
ships were used by the merchant marine. International connections were made by three-
masters, *full-rigged* and *bark*; by two-masters,
the *brigantine*, the *brig* and the *schooner*; and
by a hybrid of the brig and the brigantine, the
snow, designed for speed. The three-masters
and the large brigantines were used for the
main transatlantic crossings, while the brigs
and smaller brigantines and the snows took
care of cabotage to the United States and the
Caribbean.

The most common craft in the Gulf of St.
Lawrence and the estuary were *sloops* (*cutters*)
or *schooners*.

Further upstream, *flat-bottomed boats*,
decked boats, *large sloops* and *Basque-style
fishing boats* were most commonly seen. All of
these craft were well suited to the sailing conditions. Their shallow draught enabled them
to sail in the waters of the river and its tribu-
taries. These vessels could have one, two or
three masts and they could be steered using

oars. They were very slow, however: it took
three or four days and sometimes as many as
six to get from Montréal to Quebec City. Fur-
thermore, navigating under sail has always
been difficult in the waters of the St. Lawrence. In spite of the prevailing (but unreli-
able) winds blowing from the west, and the
pull of the current downstream, the tide below Trois-Rivières still slows ships down.

CANADIAN Illustrated News

Vol. XX.—No. 2.   MONTREAL, SATURDAY, JULY 12, 1879.   SINGLE COPIES, TEN CENTS. $4 PER YEAR IN ADVANCE.

AROUND 1870, SAILING SHIPS AND STEAMSHIPS MINGLE IN KING'S BASIN NEXT TO ISLAND QUAY.

THEIR SQUARE SAILS FILLED BY THE WESTERLY WIND, BARGES LOADED WITH HAY BREAST THE STRONG ST. MARY'S CURRENT IN 1879.

TWO BARGES NEAR MONTRÉAL, AROUND 1915. ONE OF THEM IS SQUARE-RIGGED.

IN THIS 1887 DRAWING, THE
QUAYS OF MONTRÉAL ARE
INCORRECTLY PORTRAYED.
NONETHELESS, THE ARTIST
HAS VERY CLEARLY SHOWN
THE LINK THAT EXISTED
FROM 1871 ON BETWEEN THE
BOATS AND THE TRAINS ON
THE QUAYS. INTERMODAL
TRANSPORT AT WORK!

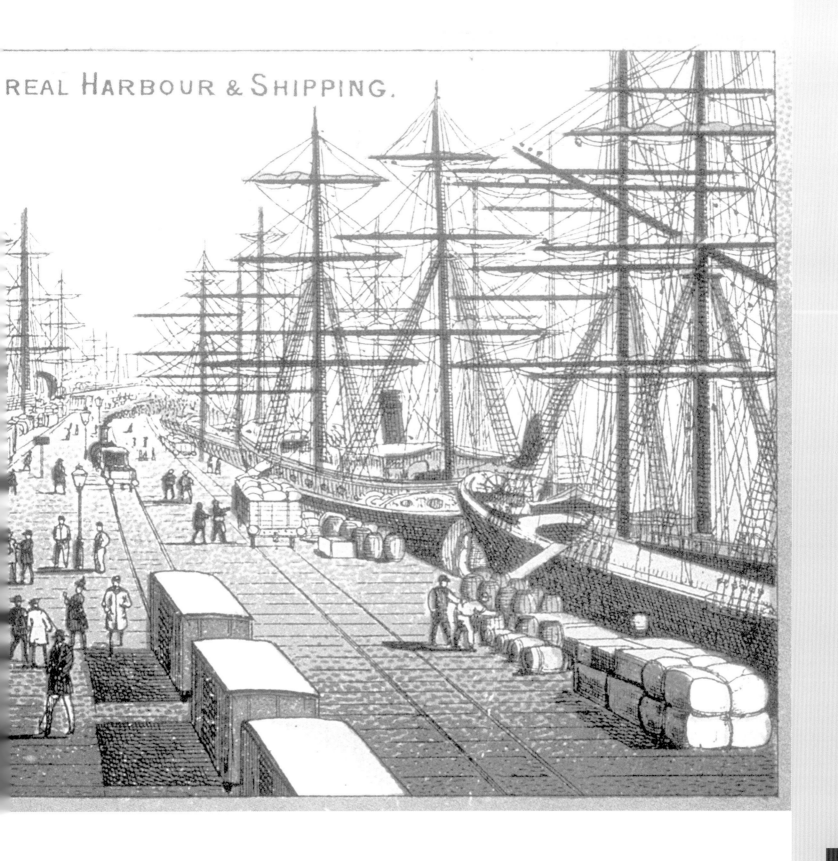

1897

2006

Then and now

Nowadays, who would suspect that the space between De la Commune Street and the St. Lawrence River was once the landing place for barges with sails?

RIGHT
CROSSING THE RAPIDS
IN A STEAMBOAT IS NOT
A RELAXING EXPERIENCE.
EXPEDITIONS LIKE THIS
DO HOWEVER TAKE PLACE.

BELOW LEFT
A PADDLE-STEAMER WITH
TWO FUNNELS, IN 1875.

BELOW RIGHT
A PADDLE-STEAMER WITH
ONE FUNNEL, IN 1885.

With sail and . . . steam

Until the nineteenth century it was very difficult to sail upstream beyond Quebec City. However, a key invention, the steam engine, was to enable Montréal to move into the ranks of the main international ports. No longer would it be necessary to wait until the winds and currents were favourable! With steam produced in a furnace continually stoked with wood or coal, a large paddle wheel could be turned to propel the boat. From then on, more regular transportation and delivery schedules could be established.

As with all innovations, the change from sail to steam was gradual and the first steamships continued to rely on sails as back-up. The first steamship to sail on the St. Lawrence River was the *Accommodation*, launched by brewer John Molson on August 19, 1809, from the Hart-Logan shipyard next to his Montréal brewery. The boat took slightly under three days—36 hours of sailing—to go from Montréal to Quebec City, and seven days to return. This was quite a feat as until then it was often necessary to wait several days, or even a week, for a favourable wind to pick up below St. Mary's current so that a boat could enter the port of Montréal.

Ten years later, the American ship *Savannah* became the first steamship to cross the Atlantic. Like the *Accommodation*, it was a hybrid, using both sails and steam. In 1833, a Canadian ship, the *Royal William*, owned by Samuel Cunard of Halifax—the founder of the Cunard Line—completed the first transatlantic crossing in just twenty-two days, using only steam. Nonetheless, the old ships were not replaced overnight, and it was on board another hybrid ship, the *SS Clyde*, that the Russell family, whom we met earlier in this book, arrived in Montréal on August 6, 1857.

1899

1897 | Around 1900

The TALBOT, one of Her
Majesty's steamships.

A seventeenth-century invention

In 1687, a French inventor, Denis Papin, developed a steam piston engine, and in 1707 he built a paddlewheel boat. In 1776, another Frenchman, engineer Jouffroy d'Abbans, designed the very first steamship to actually sail. The commercial use of the steamship began in France in 1783 on the Saône and in America in 1787 on the Delaware.

UPPER
THE BAVARIA, OF THE
ALLAN SHIPPING LINE.

MIDDLE
A STEAMSHIP ALONGSIDE
A THREE-MASTER IN THE
PORT OF MONTRÉAL.

LOWER
THE NORONIC, A SCREW-
PROPELLER STEAMSHIP
BELONGING TO CANADA
STEAMSHIP LINES.

Around 1915

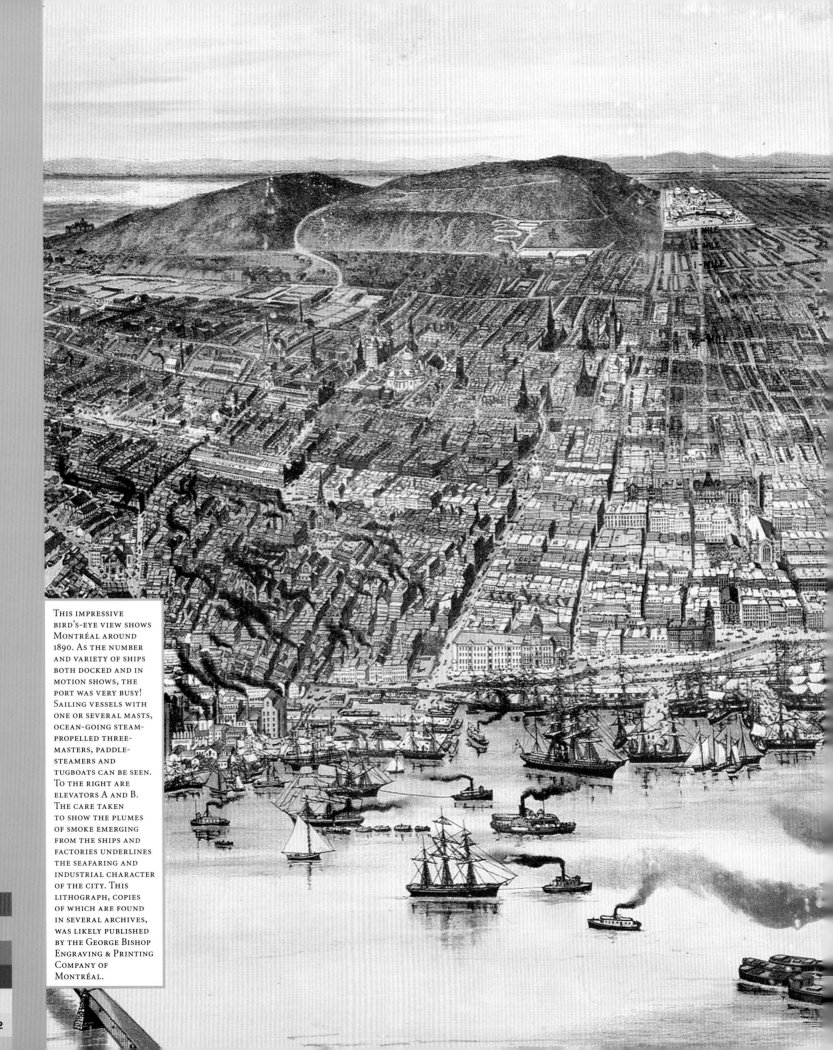

THIS IMPRESSIVE BIRD'S-EYE VIEW SHOWS MONTRÉAL AROUND 1890. AS THE NUMBER AND VARIETY OF SHIPS BOTH DOCKED AND IN MOTION SHOWS, THE PORT WAS VERY BUSY! SAILING VESSELS WITH ONE OR SEVERAL MASTS, OCEAN-GOING STEAM-PROPELLED THREE-MASTERS, PADDLE-STEAMERS AND TUGBOATS CAN BE SEEN. TO THE RIGHT ARE ELEVATORS A AND B. THE CARE TAKEN TO SHOW THE PLUMES OF SMOKE EMERGING FROM THE SHIPS AND FACTORIES UNDERLINES THE SEAFARING AND INDUSTRIAL CHARACTER OF THE CITY. THIS LITHOGRAPH, COPIES OF WHICH ARE FOUND IN SEVERAL ARCHIVES, WAS LIKELY PUBLISHED BY THE GEORGE BISHOP ENGRAVING & PRINTING COMPANY OF MONTRÉAL.

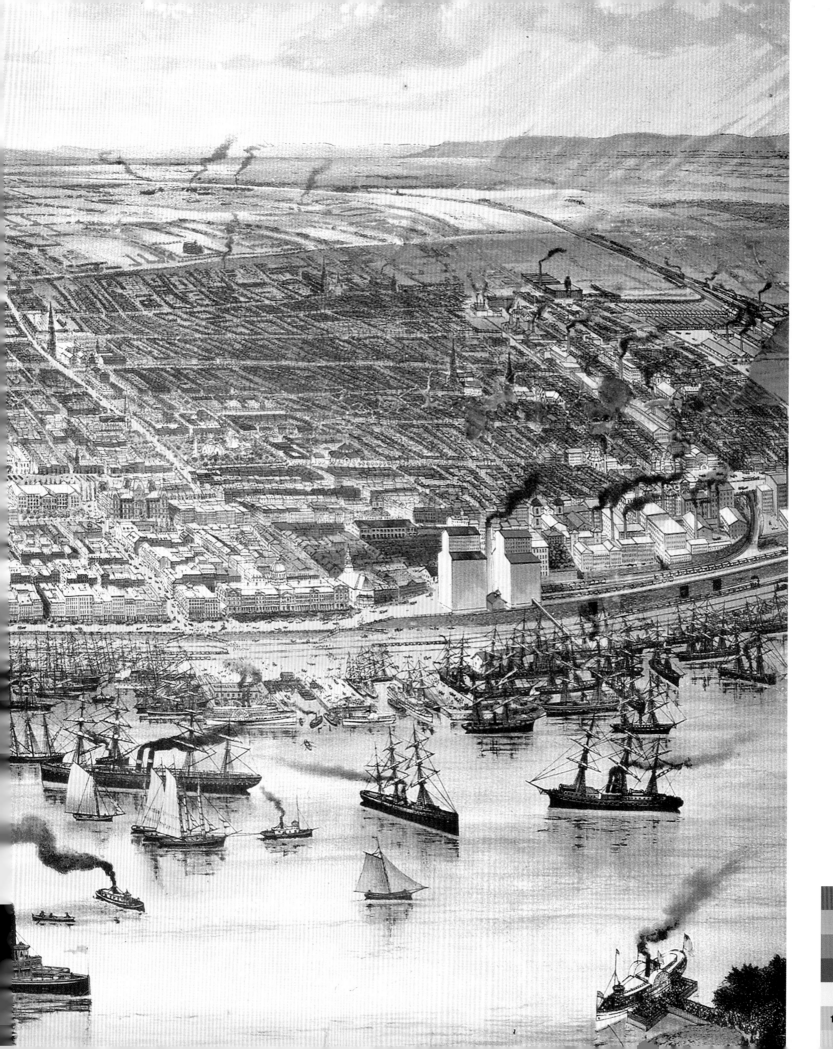

The shipping companies

SIR HUGH ALLAN,
A CANADIAN SHIPPING
MAGNATE OF THE
NINETEENTH CENTURY.

The history of the port of Montréal is also that of the shipping companies that located here. One of the first was the Edmonstone, Allan & Company, renamed in 1835 when Hugh Allan joined its ranks. In 1858, the company built for its own use the "Allan Building", now occupied by the Old Port of Montréal Corporation.

In the middle of the nineteenth century, several shipping companies fought a tough battle to control navigation on the St. Lawrence River and international trade. Among these were the Montréal Ocean Steamship Company, known as the Allan Line, and its rival, the Canadian Steam Navigation Company. These were the first to establish a regular service to England. The Allan Line soon had a monopoly, however, supported by government subsidies. Because of its superior ships built in Scotland—steamboats with propellers and iron hulls—it could offer direct steamship service, leaving every two weeks, between Montréal and Liverpool during the summer, and between Portland and Liverpool from November to May. It carried immigrants and goods and provided regular mail service. In 1870, the Allan Line secured a contract for the transportation of "subsidized passengers", who were guaranteed land or work, as well as a train ticket to the Canadian West on the Grand Trunk Railway. The main shareholder was Sir Hugh Allan, a Scot by birth. His company, which underwent several name changes, was finally taken over in 1909 by Canadian Pacific and in 1915 was merged into Canadian Pacific Ocean Services Ltd.

Sir Hugh Allan was also the first president of a river navigation company, the Richelieu & Ontario Navigation Company, created in 1874 by the merger of the Richelieu Company and the Canadian Steam Navigation Company. This merger gave him total control over shipping in the St. Lawrence, from Tadoussac to Lake Ontario and Toronto. Later, in 1913, this company joined with others to form the famous Canada Steamship Lines. The company would go on to operate cruise ships on the St. Lawrence River. Among these were the "white ships"—so called by people living along the river because of the ships' colour—that sailed to the Manoir Richelieu in the Charlevoix region, as well as through the Lachine Rapids. The Richelieu Company and the Allan Line were the first companies to occupy sheds on the quays of Montréal.

But Sir Hugh had many competitors. Among them was Samuel Cunard, owner of the British & North American Royal Mail Steamship Company, which became the Cunard Steamship Line. In 1957, the Cunard Steamship Line bought out the White Star Line (with which it had first merged to form the Cunard White Star Line), a shipping company founded in 1845 in Liverpool and one of the most important of the early twentieth century. However, after having built the largest liners in the world, including the Titanic, the White Star fell into serious financial difficulties. Note that the Cunard line still offers cruises all over the world.

These companies occupied sheds in the port of Montréal until the early 1970s. Today, only transatlantic ships and cruise ships continue to dock at the quays, where in the 1960s two passenger terminals, Louis Joliet Terminal on King Edward Quay and Iberville Terminal on Alexandra Quay, were located. The latter is still used as a passenger terminal, under the management of the Montréal Port Authority.

Around 1900

1888

1889-1890

2006

Then and now

THE PORT IN THE
NINETEENTH CENTURY,
JUST BEFORE THE CURRENT
QUAYS WERE BUILT, AND
AS IT NOW APPEARS. THE
TOWERS OF NOTRE-DAME
BASILICA SHOW THAT THE
TWO PICTURES ARE OF THE
SAME AREA. IN THE PHOTO
ON THE RIGHT, NOTE THE
RAILWAY BRIDGE.

The first ship of the season

In 1840, the Montréal Harbour Commission, at the instigation of its third president, J.-G. MacKenzie, established an award to be given to the first ship of the year to dock in the port of Montréal. The "Gold-Headed Cane" was created to encourage ship owners to resume regular connections with Montréal as early in the season as possible: the closing of the port in winter because of ice on the river put it at a disadvantage with respect to other ports on the Atlantic.

The strategy worked beautifully. Right from the earliest years of the competition, there was intense rivalry among sea captains: they all wanted to win the coveted award.

Up to 1960, it was not until April that the first ships could make it up the St. Lawrence to Montréal. Since then, with the help of ice-breakers, the winner docks in Montréal as early as January—the first to do so was the Danish cargo ship *Helga Dan*, on January 4, 1964—and often as early as New Year's Day.

At one time, ocean-going vessels from the east coast of the United States participated in the competition—without having made the rough Atlantic crossing, which put the Europeans at a disadvantage. As a result, the commissioners created a prize specifically for this first group, the Top-Hat. However, after 1880 only the Gold-Headed Cane was awarded.

In the nineteenth century, passenger ships almost always won the prize. Since 1914, the Gold-Headed Cane has also been won by cargo ships, two of which were oil tankers, the *Acardo* in 1931 and the *Golden Eagle* in 1971. From 1840 to 1940, ninety English ships were awarded the prize. The record number of wins is held by the *Great Britain II*, which won the prize six times between 1840 and 1850. In the twentieth century, only Captain Roger Llewellyn has won the Cane three times over.

In recent decades, the winners have come from many different countries.

CAPTAIN E. A. LEBLANC OF THE *LADY RODNEY*, RECEIVES THE GOLD-HEADED CANE FROM THE PORT MANAGER, ALEX FERGUSON.

1940

The Gold-Headed Cane

Sometimes the Gold-Headed Cane is straight, and sometimes it has a curved handle. In some years the captain can choose between two styles.

Today's trophy is an elegant ceremonial cane made of hardwood finished with a dark brown varnish. About 80 centimeters long, its smooth, straight body tapers from the famous Gold Head to a recently added gold tip. The 14-karat Gold Head, about four centimeters high and 3.5 centimeters in diameter at its widest, is crowned with a relief Canadian coat-of-arms coloured with inlaid enamel. An inscription around the side reads: "Presented by the Port of Montréal to (captain's name), Master of the (ship's name), the first ocean-going vessel in the Port in (year)."

PORT OF MONTRÉAL, the Gold-Headed Cane, 1988

The recipients of the Gold-Headed Cane, 1998-2007

Source: Archives – Port of Montréal

YEAR	SHIP	NATIONALITY	CAPTAIN
1998	Canmar Valour	British / Bermuda	Spacal, Davor
1999	OOCL Belgium	Chinese	Llewellyn, Roger
2000	Aqua Stoli	Maltese	Gudkov, Volodymyr
2001	P&O Nedlloyd Ottawa	Marshall Islands	Schuessler, Dietrich
2002	Canmar Glory	Bermuda	Comor, Omer
2003	Canmar Courage	Bermuda	Engineer, Ashwani K.
2004	Canmar Triumph	Bermuda	Franic, Branimir
2005	MSC Brianna	Panama	Alessandrelli, Aroldo
2006	CP Bravery	Bermuda	Krzanic, Tonci
2007	Glory	Bermuda	Saldanha, Oswald Pascal

ICE-BREAKERS SUCH AS THE *LADY GREY*, SEEN AT WORK HERE IN 1910, WERE FIRST USED ON THE ST. LAWRENCE AT THE BEGINNING OF THE TWENTIETH CENTURY AND ALLOWED THE SHIPPING SEASON TO BE GRADUALLY EXTENDED. AFTER 1960, THEIR USE MEANT THAT THE CHANNEL AND THE PORT OF MONTRÉAL COULD STAY OPEN ALL YEAR LONG.

May 9, 1874

BEFORE THE STEAM ENGINE
WAS INVENTED, OXEN,
HORSES OR MULES TOWED
THE SHIPS WHEN A LACK
OF WIND PREVENTED THEM
FROM SAILING AGAINST
THE STRONG ST. MARY'S
CURRENT BLOCKING THE
ENTRANCE TO THE PORT OF
MONTRÉAL—A FREQUENT
OCCURRENCE.

The indispensable and gallant tugboats

Today, in Basin 1 north of the Lachine Canal, the *Daniel McAllister*, sitting on its concrete pad, is a reminder of a centuries-old activity in the port of Montréal: towing. It's not easy to sail against St. Mary's current when you are a sailing ship and there is no wind . . . Tugboats also assist the huge ocean-going ships with their docking manoeuvres. They also tow barges on the river, just as they towed the cages in the nineteenth century.

The first tugboats, small light boats with a high powered engine (from 600 to 1000 horse-power), came into use with the development of the steam engine. They were very busy on the Lachine Canal in the days of the great sailing ships, as these could not manoeuvre easily in the port or in the canal.

The Harbour Commissioners were the first owners of the towing—and dredging—fleet. For several generations, the McAllister fam-

ily had a monopoly over these services. The port of Montréal authorities have also owned several tugboats equipped with pumps for fighting fires. In New York, a fire boat still makes a spectacular appearance during official ceremonies.

SOME TUGBOATS WERE
EQUIPPED WITH PUMPS
FOR FIRE-FIGHTING ON THE
WATER OR ON THE QUAYS.
HERE, THE *ST. PETER*,
AROUND 1910.

Two small shoals lying off the west end of it, at the entrance of the harbor [of Montréal], and the narrowness of the deep water channel below it, generally make it necessary to warp out large ships and drop them down the stream by kedge-anchors until they come abreast of the new market-place as the leading winds for bringing them out cannot always be depended upon: at the east end of the island is a channel, of which small craft can always avail themselves. The greatest disadvantage to this harbour is the rapid of St. Mary about a mile below it, whose current is so powerful that without a strong north-easterly wind, ships cannot stern it and would sometimes be detained even for weeks about two miles only from the place where they are to deliver their freight.

JOSEPH BOUCHETTE, 1815 (1832)

The towing fleet belonging to the Montréal Harbour Commissioners, around 1930.

The tugboat *Daniel McAllister*, anchored near the first locks, was recognized as being of exceptional interest by the Canadian Cultural Property Export Review Board. It awaits restoration.

Tugboats are still indispensable for guiding ships around ports.

The Lachine Canal

When the Lachine Canal was being built, between 1821 and 1826, three staircase locks (on the right in this drawing) were constructed at the downstream entrance where the fall was greatest. When the canal had to be widened, between 1843 and 1848, two additional locks were built on the north side, so as to maintain traffic during construction—these are now locks 1 and 2 (on the left). The oldest locks were eventually replaced around 1879 by the current south series, each of which measures 270 feet in length rather than the original 100 feet. In 1904, the north locks were in turn lengthened from 200 to 270 feet, as this had become the standard length for canal navigation.

In this first image of the downstream entrance around 1850—an illustration that Benoît Léonard was commissioned to produce in 1993 and that was based on recently acquired archaeological data—a steamship has just passed through lock 2 on the north side. On the right, can be seen the windmill after which the point of land was named and the house where the lock operator and his family lived at the time.

The gateway to the Upper St. Lawrence

At the western end of the Old Port are located the oldest remains of an amazing work of canalization officially inaugurated on August 24, 1824—the Lachine Canal.

Gateway to the canal network that would eventually connect the Atlantic to the heart of the North American continent, and one of its oldest links, the canal solved the navigation problems responsible in large part for hindering the development of Montréal—and indeed of Canada as a whole. From then on, the Lachine Rapids, with a drop of 14 metres between Lake St. Louis, at Lachine, and the St. Lawrence in Montréal, no longer posed any danger to ships heading for the Great Lakes.

With a length of 14.5 kilometres, the canal is composed of five stretches of water or *reaches,* of various lengths and levels, which a boat sails into—or out of—through a lock

chamber that acts as a step: the chamber allows the boat to move up or down to reach the next stretch of water. Let's take a quick look back at the canal's history.

From 1689 until 1701, the Sulpicians, the "seigneurs" (or landowners) of the island of Montréal, began to dig a navigable canal that would bypass the Sault St. Louis—the Lachine Rapids—and at the same time carry water to power their flour mills. In the end, only the St. Gabriel segment would be completed. Flour production benefited, as predicted, but there is nothing to indicate that vessels navigated on the canal for commercial purposes.

In later years, several attempts at completing the canal failed. It was not until the beginning of the nineteenth century that all of the political and economic conditions necessary for the canalization of the Upper St. Lawrence

came together. In 1817, the construction of the Erie Canal was announced in the United States. This would allow goods arriving in Lake Erie to be transported via Buffalo, Albany and the Hudson River all the way to the port of New York. A fierce competition began between New York and the port of Montréal for the Great Lakes market . . . Thanks to the efforts of Montréal's merchants and assistance from the governments of Lower Canada and Great Britain, the vital Lachine Canal was officially opened in 1824. One year ahead of its competitor!

Although today we commonly refer to the "1825 canal", it was only during the 1826 season that vessels could travel its *entire* length, just one season later than on the Erie Canal. The Lachine Canal was such a success that it soon had to be widened, not once but twice.

View of Barges looking east.

Painting the Figurehead.

IN THE SPRING, THE CANAL WAS EMPTIED FOR CLEANING AND IT WAS A GOOD TIME TO REPAIR BOATS. SHOWN HERE, THE CANAL DURING THE SPRING OF 1876.

*O*ld Montréal is located just downstream from a major system of rapids that impede entry to the great waterways leading into the heart of North America. The Lachine Rapids are the first in the system as you head west and this natural obstacle has made the harbour of Montréal a transit hub for commercial activity in Canada and across the continent.

GILLES ROUSSEAU, 2007 (free translation)

IN THE NINETEENTH CENTURY, CANAL EXCAVATION—LIKE THAT OF THE LACHINE CANAL ILLUSTRATED HERE—WAS COMPARABLE IN MAGNITUDE TO THE CONSTRUCTION OF HYDROELECTRIC DAMS IN THE TWENTIETH CENTURY.

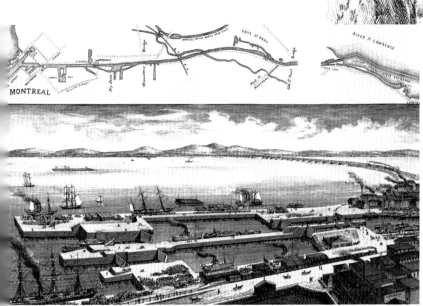

MONTREAL

IN 1877, NEW CONSTRUCTION WAS BEGUN TO FURTHER IMPROVE THE CANAL'S OPERATIONS. IT WOULD TAKE 12 YEARS TO COMPLETE. IN 1885, THE OLD STAIRCASE LOCKS (NO TRACE OF WHICH REMAINS TODAY) WERE REPLACED BY NEWER ONES. THESE NOW ACT AS SPILLWAYS ON THE SOUTH SIDE; WATER FLOWING OVER THEM HELPS OXYGENATE AND THUS PURIFY THE WATER. ONLY LOCKS 1 AND 2 (ON THE NORTH SIDE) ARE USED TODAY BY PLEASURE CRAFT. SIMILARLY ONLY ONE LOCK AT EACH REACH IS CURRENTLY IN USE UPSTREAM.

The ingenious lock

A lock is an airlocked chamber that acts like a step on a staircase. Its purpose: to enable a boat to move from one level to another between two adjacent stretches of water (reaches) in a canal or on a canalized river.

The principle that makes a lock work is both simple and efficient. At each end there are *gates* with valves (openings) which, when opened or closed in a controlled sequence, allow the *lock chamber* where the boat is located to be filled or emptied.

When a boat has to be raised from the downstream reach to the upstream reach (westward), the lock operator opens the downstream gates, the boat sails in and the downstream gates close behind it. Then the upstream valves are opened—with the gates themselves remaining closed. As the water flows in naturally from the upper reach, it fills the lock chamber and the boat gently rises. When the level is the same as the upper stretch of water, the upstream gates are opened and the boat can go on its way.

If instead the boat is travelling downstream (eastward), the process is reversed.

Passage through the lock is called *lockage*. On the canal, the passage through each lock takes 15 to 30 minutes (25 minutes in locks 1 and 2). In the St. Lawrence Seaway, the process requires a little more than half an hour—the time it takes to displace some 91 million litres of water! These locks also differ from those in the Lachine Canal in that the valves are not located at the base of the gates: the lock chambers are instead filled or emptied using a culvert system built into the side walls of the lock chamber.

THE HYDRAULIC PRINCIPLES ON WHICH CANALS WITH LOCKS ARE BASED WERE DEVELOPED AS EARLY AS THE FIFTEENTH CENTURY. THE *ENCYCLOPEDIA* OF DIDEROT AND D'ALEMBERT, PUBLISHED IN 1762, EXPLAINS HOW A LOCK WORKS—SHOWN BELOW BY A *LOCKAGE* ON THE LACHINE CANAL.

❶ THE BOAT ENTERS THE LOCK AT THE LEVEL OF THE RIVER.

❷ ONCE THE DOWNSTREAM GATE HAS BEEN CLOSED, THE LOCK CHAMBER IS FILLED UP: THE BOAT RISES.

❸ THE BOAT LEAVES THE LOCK AT THE LEVEL OF THE UPPER REACH.

IN THE FOREGROUND, THE DOWNSTREAM ENTRANCE TO LOCK 1, WITH ITS RESTORED CURVED WALLS AND THE REMAINS OF THE STAIRS ADDED IN THE TWENTIETH CENTURY. IN THE BACKGROUND, THE LOCKKEEPER'S DWELLING, WHOSE SHAPE ECHOES THAT OF THE ELEVATORS THAT CAN BE SEEN IN THE DISTANCE.

PARTLY VISIBLE HERE ON THE LEFT, THE ROTUNDA, A STONE WALL CURVED LIKE THE ARC OF A CIRCLE, MARKS THE END OF THE SMALL ISLAND BETWEEN THE SOUTH AND NORTH LOCKS (THE LOCK GARDENS).

A UNIQUE ARCHITECTURAL STRUCTURE ON THE CANAL, THE ROTUNDA WAS NO DOUBT BUILT TO PROTECT THE DOWNSTREAM ENTRANCE FROM DAMAGE CAUSED BY ICE WHICH, THROUGHOUT THE NINETEENTH CENTURY, FREQUENTLY SWEPT AWAY OR DAMAGED THE QUAY THAT WAS LOCATED THERE. THE ROTUNDA WAS COMPLETELY RESTORED IN 1991, WITH THE ONE DIFFERENCE THAT THE SURFACES OF THE NEW STONES ARE NOT DRESSED (PITTED WITH SMALL INDENTATIONS AND BORDERED WITH SHALLOW GROOVES). WE CAN NOW DISTINGUISH BETWEEN THE ORIGINAL WORK AND THE RESTORATION.

A VIEW OF THE ROTUNDA BY NIGHT—IN THE CENTRE.

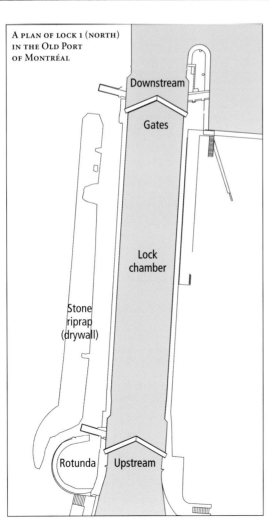

A PLAN OF LOCK 1 (NORTH) IN THE OLD PORT OF MONTRÉAL

Downstream

Gates

Lock chamber

Stone riprap (drywall)

Rotunda   Upstream

At the downstream entrance to the canal, floating elevators were used for transshipping grain from boats arriving from the west onto schooners and ocean liners heading eastward. In the foreground, a crank winch (here the crank is leaning against the winch) is used to manually open and close the gates of lock 1. The Electricity Fairy hasn't arrived yet . . . An onlooker, perhaps the lock operator, sits on the rotunda and looks out over the port.

FILLING A LOCK, HERE
BEING WATCHED OVER
BY THE OLD PORT OF
MONTRÉAL'S LOCK
OPERATOR, USED TO
CAUSE MUCH MORE
TURBULENCE THAN THIS!
WHEN LOCKS 1 AND 2
WERE RESTORED,
HYDRAULIC STUDIES ON
SCALE MODELS SHOWED
THAT IT WAS NECESSARY
TO INSTALL A DEVICE
TO DECREASE THE
TURBULENCE AND THUS
ALLOW SMALL CRAFT TO
USE THE LOCK CHAMBERS
SAFELY—THIS WAS
SUBSEQUENTLY DONE.
NOTICE AS WELL IN
THIS PHOTOGRAPH THE
MITRE GATES: CLOSING
THE GATES AT AN ANGLE
RATHER THAN IN
A STRAIGHT LINE
CONSIDERABLY
STRENGTHENS THEIR
RESISTANCE TO WATER
PRESSURE AND PREVENTS
THE GATES FROM
OPENING ACCIDENTALLY
BEFORE THE WATER IN
THE LOCK CHAMBER
RISES TO THE LEVEL
OF THAT IN THE
EXIT REACH.

A navigable corridor . . .

Right from when it opened, the Lachine Canal proved to be a vital communications and transport link to the heart of the country. Already, in 1826, 1,300 ships went through the locks. In 1850, there were 6,169, carrying nearly 60,000 passengers. During the same period, the port of Montréal acquired the infrastructure necessary to handle barges, goods and passengers from riverboats and ocean-going ships and, later on, canal boats.

Throughout the navigation season, the downstream entrance thus became a site of intense transhipping activity, in both directions. Soon, sea traffic became so heavy that the authorities decided to double the width of the canal—work that was carried out between 1843 and 1848. So as not to interrupt traffic during this period, new locks were built parallel to the old ones. Five locks were built to handle the difference in water level between Montréal and Lachine, as compared to the original seven, which nonetheless remained open to lighter boats for some time.

Early on, Montréal's old upper lock was put to a different use: it became a dry dock for boat repair. It was a simple matter to empty the lock chamber and repaint a hull when it was dry, and then refill the chamber when the boat was ready to sail again. During the 1850s, brothers George and William Tate located their dry docks at the western end of basin 2, near spillway 2, under what is now the Bonaventure Autoroute. These were used until the beginning of the 1960s.

The canal was again lengthened and deepened between 1873 and 1885.

BARGES LOADED WITH COAL WAIT TO BE TOWED ON THE CANAL. IN THE BACKGROUND, THE OLDEST SECTION OF ELEVATOR 5. CONVEYOR GALLERIES WERE LOCATED ON THE QUAY WHERE CONCRETE ELEVATORS NOW STAND.

Around 1910

. . . that became a source of energy and water

It was not long before the Lachine Canal became more than just a navigable corridor. As soon as it was widened the first time, it began to contribute greatly to economic development, as factories that wanted to locate on its banks were granted leases to use the water—mainly to generate hydraulic energy but also to feed steam engines and to meet manufacturing needs, as in the case of the Redpath refinery near the St. Gabriel Locks. Indeed, from the early days of industrialization right up to the Second World War, the canal's industrial corridor was one of the main manufacturing centres in Canada.

A word of explanation: Widening the canal caused the volume of water flowing through the locks to increase. This gave the port authorities the idea, as was being done in several industrial complexes in New England, of putting the hydraulic energy flowing from these artificial waterfalls to use: openings built into the walls or into the banks of the canal carried the water into the factories to turn wheels or turbines which, using a gear shaft and a set of gear wheels, pulleys and straps, would power the machines. Note that we are referring here to direct-drive waterpower and not to hydroelectricity. The latter was only produced along the canal after 1887, first mainly for lighting and then gradually—when the

hydroelectric plant on the Côte-Saint-Paul was built (1903-1904)—to open and close the locks and to operate vertical-lift bridges and swing bridges along the waterway, a manoeuvre that had until then been done manually. From 1910 on, however, industries turned more and more to electricity—either generated by their own turbines or coming from the distribution network.

The government charged a fair price for these "hydraulic rights", guaranteed energy whose source was located right near the city and whose power was comparable to that of the water-powered industrial centres of New England. The first leases were granted in 1846 alongside basin 2—between what is now the Mill Street Bridge and the Bonaventure Autoroute. The strip of land between this basin

and the river did in fact have the best conditions for waterpower development: the combined difference in level of locks 1 and 2 was more than 7 metres! Iron foundries and nailworks, large consumers of energy and water, were among the first to locate there, along with flour mills, which in 1860 produced nearly 60% of the flour consumed in Quebec—some are still there today.

Later, the locks further upstream, namely the St. Gabriel Locks (locks 3, also called the Seigneurs' Locks) and the Côte-Saint-Paul Locks (locks 4), were harnessed as well, in 1851 and 1853 respectively. But whereas in basin 2, simple government leases permitted each industrialist to use the hydraulic energy, at the St. Gabriel Locks these rights were handed over to a consortium that included John Young, the President of the Montréal Harbour Commission. At Côte-Saint-Paul, another formula was used, in which the owner rented land, energy and water all at the same time. A real "package deal"!

From closure to rebirth

In 1959, the opening of the St. Lawrence Seaway signalled the closing of the Lachine Canal. This happened gradually, starting in Montréal.

The decrease in grain-handling activity and a more diverse range of goods in transit led over time to transshipment from boat to boat and the use of containers, for which storage and handling space then had to be found. The port authorities, who had just filled in Bonsecours Basin, intending to use this new space for a container terminal, then did the same at the downstream entrance to the canal. In the end, three terminals would eventually be built further east, with the spaces originally designated remaining more or less open.

The canal, which in 1929 had been declared a site of national historic interest by the Historic Sites and Monuments Board of Canada, was officially closed to all navigation in 1970. There would soon be more changes.

The section to the east of the Bonaventure Autoroute, which came under the jurisdiction of National Ports in 1965, was transferred to the Old Port of Montréal Corporation in 1984. The Corporation put the clearing of locks 1 and 2 on its agenda. They were reopened to navigation in 1992.

The section to the west of the autoroute, on the other hand, was given in 1974 to the federal Department of Public Works, which laid out a bicycle path along the canal. In 1978, Parks Canada was given the mandate to develop its cultural and recreational potential. Historical studies carried out at the time led in 1996 to the designation of the industrial corridor as a Canadian national historic site. Finally, in 1997, as the Old Port of Montréal had done with its first two locks, Parks Canada began to restore the rest, with the intent of

1984-1985. LOCKS 1 AND 2 ARE BEING CLEARED OUT. THE LOCKS WERE LENGTHENED AND WIDENED IN 1848, REPAIRED AND LENGTHENED AGAIN AROUND 1905, THEN FILLED IN BETWEEN 1965 AND 1967.

reopening the canal for pleasure boating. As a result, since 2002, many pleasure craft have been able to travel the full length of this peaceful waterway to bypass the Lachine Rapids, without having to go through the huge Seaway locks.

EVEN THOUGH MANY OF THE CANAL'S FORMER FACILITIES HAVE BEEN DEMOLISHED, TRACES OF THEM REMAIN UNDERGROUND, FOR EXAMPLE, FOUNDATIONS OF INDUSTRIAL BUILDINGS, SLUICES, PENSTOCKS AND AT THE END, *HYDRAULIC TURBINES* LIKE THIS ONE, DISCOVERED IN 1993 ON THE SITE OF THE ROZON FLOUR MILL.

Traces remaining

During restoration work on locks 1 and 2, undertaken between 1990 and 1992 by the Old Port of Montréal Corporation, several archaeological remains were uncovered. Some, still visible, have been integrated into new developments. Others were filled in for maintenance purposes, and a few were covered over to make way for the International Flora Montréal facilities.

As for the riverside industries along basin 2, few traces can be seen today, since the basin has not been completely cleared out: only a corridor was cleared along the north wall to allow pleasure craft to pass through. The depth of the water is a little more than two metres, compared with six metres in the days of commercial navigation.

Similarly, the locks' hydraulic energy is no longer used. Nonetheless, several industries still hold leases on the water in the canal.

LOCKS 1 AND 2 WHEN THEY
WERE REOPENED FOR
NAVIGATION IN 1992, AFTER
MAJOR REDEVELOPMENT
WORK UNDERTAKEN BY THE
OLD PORT OF MONTRÉAL.

TODAY, PARKS CANADA
RUNS AN INTERPRETATIVE
CRUISE ON *L'ÉCLUSIER* SO
THAT VISITORS CAN LEARN
ABOUT THE HISTORY OF THE
CANAL WHILE PASSING
THROUGH THE RESTORED
ST. GABRIEL LOCK.

IN 2006, THE OLD PORT
SECTOR WELCOMED THE
INTERNATIONAL FLORA
MONTRÉAL.

Dredging the port and the channel

In times past, the type of watercraft used by native peoples, their knowledge of the river system and their skill enabled them to bypass natural obstacles, but it was quite a different story for Europeans sailing on much larger ships and vessels.

GILLES ROUSSEAU, 2007 (free translation)

The construction of the Lachine Canal and other canals on the Upper St. Lawrence meant that the rapids could be bypassed, eliminating one of the main obstacles to westward navigation. However, around 1830, Montréal's harbour was still only accessible to vessels with a shallow draught. Dredging a channel was the only answer.

At the time, dredging ports was common, especially in seaports with strong tides. (As far back as the end of the fifteenth century, Leonardo de Vinci had designed a model of a dredger for deepening and cleaning out lakes and canals!) In 1832, the Montréal Harbour Commissioners bought the first major piece of equipment from Great Britain: a steam-powered dredger, or cure-môle in French (the term môle meaning a breakwater, dike or pier). However, the construction of the barge on which the machine would be installed was not authorized until 1838, which meant that the machine had to be stored for years in a shed. Fi-

nally, in 1840, dredging began around the piers in the port, which made access for larger ships easier. Nonetheless, Lake St. Pierre still imposed limits on the tonnage of ships coming from Quebec City.

The port of Montréal's territory stretched from the Lachine Rapids to Portneuf. Trinity House, the organization which had set up the first police force, had control over most of the channel between Montréal and Quebec City. It was under their authority that the first bathometric readings for the dredging of a channel in Lake St. Pierre were taken in 1830. Fourteen years later . . . , construction began, with two dredgers, two steamships and a few barges.

By about 1850, a straight channel, forty-five metres wide by three to four metres deep, allowed small sailing vessels—schooners, brigantines and brigs—to pass through. Sometime around 1865, the average depth reached six metres. As most ocean-going vessels were now able to sail through, the port of Montréal, which

saw about 20 ocean-going vessels per year around 1815, soon welcomed more than three hundred. From 1866 to 1870, taking into account the coastal boats and American ships, the number of ships per year rose to nearly 6,000!

The shipping channel continued to be modified to keep pace with increasingly large ships. At the beginning of the twentieth century, its depth and that of the berthing area reached nine, and in some places ten, metres. The port's fleet of dredgers took turns constantly maintaining the channel. Then, when the Seaway was built, the southern section of the deck of Jacques Cartier Bridge had to be raised to allow ocean-going vessels, which had both a deeper draught and rose higher above the water, to sail under the bridge.

Today, the channel is more than 11 metres in depth, deep enough for almost all ships. It now reaches the top of the Louis Hippolyte Lafontaine Tunnel—opened in 1967—which limits the draught of ships sailing west.

Several models of
dredgers were used to dig
the channel, depending
on the type of sediment.
Above, a grab dredger at
work during the
construction of Victoria
Pier (now Clock Tower
Quay). The material
removed was used to fill
in the quays and piers.

A bucket dredger
in action.

FROM TOP TO BOTTOM

A ROCK-DRILLING VESSEL—
THE DIGGING IS DONE USING
AN AUGER.

DREDGER 1 BELONGING TO
THE "NAVY DEPARTMENT",
AROUND 1910.

A GRAB DREDGER.

DREDGERS AT THE QUAY,
IN 1919.

REGULAR DREDGING
MAINTENANCE OF THE
CHANNEL AND PORT MEANS
THAT IT IS NOW POSSIBLE TO
ACCOMMODATE MOST SHIPS.

1872

THROUGH THE CENTURIES,
BOATS HAVE CONTINUED TO
DROP ANCHOR IN MONTRÉAL.

CLOCK TOWER QUAY
IS THE PERFECT PLACE
FOR ANYONE WHO LIKES
TO WHILE AWAY THE HOURS
CONTEMPLATING THE
LANDSCAPE AND THE
PASSAGE OF TIME.
ST. MARY'S CURRENT STILL
RUSHES UNDER JACQUES
CARTIER BRIDGE,
THE ISLANDS OF EXPO 67
HAVE BECOME JEAN
DRAPEAU PARK, AND
THE PORT NOW STRETCHES
FAR TO THE EAST.

Welcome aboard

The Old Port of Montréal, with all its current maritime facilities and activities, carries on the tradition of the site by offering Montrealers and tourists—as did the ferries and excursion boats of days gone by—sailing experiences that can be either relaxing or extreme. Another way to travel back and forth between yesterday and today: go on board one of the "big ships" passing through the port.

THE SEINE HAS ITS BATEAUX-MOUCHES; THE ST. LAWRENCE HAS THE *Bateau-Mouche*, ON WHICH YOU CAN DISCOVER THE PORT FACILITIES AND SEE ENVIRONMENT CANADA'S BIOSPHERE UP CLOSE.

A river for everyone

Montréal is an island, but such a large and developed one that there are very few places where this can be appreciated. The quays of the Old Port are among these places. As soon as fine weather arrives, several of the boats docked along the quays invite passers-by to sail on the waters of the river and to see Montréal and its port from a different perspective. Some of the proposed activities grew out of their promoters' love affair with the beauty of the city at sunset or out of the adrenaline rush of a kayak ride through the Lachine rapids.

The era when the port was surrounded by walls and closed to city dwellers is long past. There is a vast choice of excursions, and shuttles even let you cross the river with a bicycle while giving your legs a rest. The St. Lawrence can be convenient, romantic, historical or athletic—it's up to each of us to discover "our" river.

SINCE 1985, THE *Amphi-Bus*, AN AMPHIBIOUS BUS, HAS ALLOWED VISITORS TO DISCOVER BOTH OLD MONTRÉAL AND THE ST. LAWRENCE RIVER—FIRST IN THE SAULT NORMAND RAPIDS AND THEN JUST ABOVE ST. MARY'S CURRENT, LESS TURBULENT NOW THAN IT ONCE WAS.

In the 1990s, the Old Port offered cruises on the *Nouvelle-Orléans*, a replica of one of the first steamships that operated in the Louisiana port at the beginning of the nineteenth century. Note that the paddle wheel, a decorative feature here, is at the stern of the boat and not on the side, as is the case for the steamboat shown below. The waters of the Mississippi are much calmer than those of the St. Lawrence, especially those near the Lachine Rapids!

LACHINE RAPIDS,

Richelieu and Ontario NAVIGATION COMPANY.

Shooting the Lachine Rapids on board the *Saute-Moutons*; the experience is as exciting today as in the era of the voyageurs' canoes or the "white boats", the steamboats on which the Richelieu & Ontario Navigation Company offered equally memorable excursions from 1850 to 1885, under the expert guidance of native pilots from Kahnawake.

AML Cruises, the first to provide river excursions in Quebec, offers cruises with an historical flavour or dinner cruises to the Boucherville Islands on the *Cavalier Maxim*.

Even in less turbulent waters, the river offers plenty of thrills. Just look at the speed and 360 degree turns of the *Jet St-Laurent*, a high-speed boat.

Two river shuttles, the *Transit* and the *Tandem*, go back and forth between the Old Port, Jean Drapeau Park (St. Helen's Island) and the Longueuil Marina. A means of transport that is especially enjoyed by walkers, cyclists and in-line skaters.

As in times past, it is possible to travel between Montréal and Quebec City on the water—these days on board an ultra-modern catamaran operated by Croisières Évasion Plus.

The first commercial electrically powered boat in Canada, *Le Petit Navire* offers a pleasant trip.

A PAUSE ALONGSIDE
JACQUES CARTIER QUAY
BEFORE SETTING OUT.

Distinguished visitors

Replicas of historic boats, frigates flying the Canadian flag, research vessels arriving from the ends of the earth . . . Like the port of Montréal in the past, the Old Port regularly welcomes "important visitors" that attract crowds when they are open to the public.

Home to a variety of commemorative events

In 1992, when the 350th anniversary of the founding of Montréal was being celebrated, the Old Port welcomed a number of important boats. One of these, the cargo ship Fort St. Louis, a ship of 150 metres in length anchored at Conveyor Quay, even put on an exhibition, Transit 92. The exhibition included plays, performances and opera, and brought back to life the developments in transportation and other technologies that took place here.

AROUND 1989, *LA BELLE BLONDE* DROPPED ANCHOR AT JACQUES CARTIER QUAY. AS LOW-LEVEL GANGWAYS HAD NOT YET BEEN BUILT, VISITORS GOT ON BOARD VIA BARGES!

1893. CARAVELLES NEWLY ARRIVED IN THE PORT OF MONTRÉAL, PULLED BY STEAM-POWERED TUGBOATS. THESE BEAUTIFUL SHIPS, USED AT THE END OF THE MIDDLE AGES, WERE RECREATED AS PART OF THE 400TH ANNIVERSARY OF CHRISTOPHER COLUMBUS'S VOYAGE TO AMERICA (1492).

THE *PÉLICAN*, AN APPROXIMATE REPLICA OF THE BOAT COMMANDED BY PIERRE LE MOYNE D'IBERVILLE (1661-1706), ANCHORED AT JACQUES CARTIER QUAY IN 1992. PEOPLE WERE SO SMITTEN WITH HER THAT SHE RETURNED IN 1993 AND 1994.

IN 1992, AS PART OF THE PROGRAMMING CELEBRATING THE 350TH ANNIVERSARY OF THE FOUNDING OF MONTRÉAL, THE *BLUE NOSE II*, A REPLICA OF THE *BLUE NOSE*, A REAL FORMULA I OF THE SEA, ATTRACTED THOUSANDS OF VISITORS TO THE OLD PORT.

Training boats, and research and defence ships

The sail training ship *Half Moon* anchored on Jacques Cartier Quay in 1994.

In May 2005, the *Tromp*, a Dutch ship, sailed into the Old Port to pay homage to Canadian veterans who had participated in the liberation of Holland. In September of the same year, the schooner *Roseway*, a sail training ship that is a part of New England's maritime history, also visited the quays of Montréal, as did the *Arctic Sunrise*, belonging to the environmental organization Greenpeace, on its way back from an Antarctic voyage. In 2004 and 2007, the *Sedna IV* docked in the Old Port—a Canadian three-master 51 metres long that travels the globe doing oceanographic research and raising public awareness on environmental issues. These photographs depict other memorable visitors.

Above

The Canadian ice-breaker *NGCC Amundsen* has become the spearhead of an ambitious international research program on the Arctic ecosystem. Here she is in December 2005, docked alongside the Old Port promenade.

Left

In 2004, frigates of the North Atlantic Treaty Organization (NATO) attracted more than 13,500 people despite a rainy weekend.

White boats with three, four, five decks or more

Floating cities carrying thousands of passengers, luxurious cruise ships regularly dock at Alexandra Quay during voyages to the Caribbean or other sunny destinations.

The *Silver Whisper*.

Weighing anchor

From yesterday to tomorrow

Since the 1830s, when the first major developments were carried out, the port of Montréal has fought long and hard to earn its place among the world's great ports. To surmount natural obstacles that hindered its expansion and to expand its activities, it drew on the technical innovations of others, if it had not already invented them itself. Canalization of turbulent waters in well-travelled waterways, the adoption of steam propulsion, dredging, innovative grain transhipping systems, the revolutionary use of steel, concrete . . . Indisputably, authorities and planners, along with thousands of workers, made the most of the harbour's strategic location at the crossroads of navigable waterways leading into the hinterland, turning it into an essential stopping place for people and goods flowing west in the nineteenth century.

The original port site thus became an ever busier transit area until the 1960s, when commercial activities gradually declined and people began to think about the port's future. The port sank into a twenty-year sleep, until awakened by the Old Port of Montréal Corporation in 1981. Now this maritime city park is the most visited attraction in Montréal. The enthusiasm of Montrealers and tourists indicates clearly that, despite early public protests—or perhaps, more correctly, especially because of these protests—, the metamorphosis of the "port" of yesteryear into the "Old Port" succeeded in fulfilling the public's profound wish to renew the connections between it and the river that had been its lifeline for so long.

Today, millions of people enjoy the bustle of the Old Port, all the more so because it is entirely focussed on the future. For example, the Montréal Science Centre has begun to renew its permanent exhibitions and a dynamic marketing campaign, under the name "Quays of the Old Port", features a wealth of up-to-the-minute activities: the visit of the *Sedna IV*; the National Environment Show; the Eureka! Festival; the Araband Live Festival, presenting to the public contemporary Arab music; other events that encourage cultural exchange . . .

Montrealers are naturally concerned with preserving the oldest structures. Of course, and the Old Port Corporation is well aware of this, there is still much to do to highlight the remains of the port's history—just as this book is only the first step toward a broader and more detailed interpretation. But already, even in their dilapidated state, the visible traces to which these pages have tried to give meaning stand as eloquent reminders of our past.

Rest assured: future generations will carry on this work and in their turn propose new voyages.

Illustration credits

Amphi-Bus
p. 120, 202b

André Roy
p. 149al, ar

Anton Fercher (A.P.E.S.)
p. 135br, 137a, 204a

Benoît Chalifour
p. 14

Bibliothèque et Archives nationales du Québec
p. 32-33, 38b, 40, 50-51, 54a, 56bl, 58bl, 59cr, 61ar, 87ar, 93, 96al, 98c, 100br, 104c, 105, 109c, bl, 114, 115bl, 122, 124b, 127a, 132a, 134bl, 138ar, 139b, 156a, 159a, 160, 165ar, 166-167, 170a, 175, 179a, 190b, 191a

Centre historique des Archives nationales de France
p. 30: Plan de la ville de Montréal par Chaussegros de Léry, 1717. (FR CAOM 03DFC472B)

p. 73b: Pavillon du Canada, Exposition universelle, Paris, 1937. (F12 12116) © Photo H. Baranger

City of Montréal, Records Management and Archives
p. 134br, 180a

Denis Farley
p. 147

ExMachina
p. 136b

Gerry Burnett
p. 112-113

International Mosaiculture of Montréal
p. 142, 143al, ac, ar

Jet Boating St-Laurent
p. 204c

John S. Metcalf Co. Limited, Grain Elevators
p. 70ar, cr

Library and Archives Canada
p. 28: Source: Library and Archives Canada's website (www.collectionscanada.gc.ca)

p. 110ar: Source: Library and Archives Canada / C-003904

p. 126a: Source: Library and Archives Canada / C-006738

p. 104bl: Source: Library and Archives Canada / C-076736

p. 126b: Source: Library and Archives Canada / C-082839

p.159b: Source: Library and Archives Canada / C-000506

p. 161b: Source: Library and Archives Canada / C-001268

p. 190a: Source: Library and Archives Canada / C-082835

p. 183c: Source: Library and Archives Canada / C-064628

p.183a: Source: Library and Archives Canada / C-064338

Lise Bousquet
p. 116, 117al, ar

Marie-Reine Mattera
p. 118a, 119b, 202b

McCord Museum
p. 26bl: Print - *An East View of Montreal, in Canada,* Thomas Patten, 1762, 18th century, M19848 © McCord Museum

p. 26br: Map - *City of Montreal,* Anonymous, 1888, 19th century, M4824 © McCord Museum

p. 27bl: Photograph - *glass lantern slide, Aerial view of harbour, Montreal, QC, about 1930,* Fairchild Aerial Surveys Co. Ltd., about 1930, 20th century, MP-0000.25.212 © McCord Museum

p. 29: Print - *The Founding of Montreal,* Donald Kenneth Anderson, about 1967, 20th century, M976.179.3 © McCord Museum

p. 31a: Painting - *The North West View of Montreal,* Richard Dillon, about 1800, 19th century, M2001.106.2 © McCord Museum

p. 34-35: Print - *Montréal,* Anonymous, about 1860, 19th century, M965.39.6 © McCord Museum

p. 36a: Photograph - *James McGill's warehouse, north west corner St. Lawrence & Commissioners Streets, Montreal, QC, 1934,* Edgar Gariépy, about 1910, 20th century, MP-0000.1777.3 © McCord Museum

p. 36b: Photograph - *Montreal harbour near Custom House, QC, 1865-75,* Alexander Henderson, 1865-1875, 19th century, MP-0000.1452.51 © McCord Museum

p. 38a: Photograph - *Ice shove, Montreal, QC, 1860-70,* Anonymous, 1860-1870, 19th century, MP-1984.107.152 © McCord Museum

p. 38c: Photograph - *Ice shove at City Hall (Bonsecours Market), Montreal, QC, 1873-74,* Alexander Henderson, 1873-1874, 19th century, MP-0000.1452.49 © McCord Museum

p. 39 PHOTO #1: Photograph - *Flood, Saint Paul near Saint Peter St., Montreal, QC, 1869,* James Inglis, 1869, 19th century, MP-0000.2888 © McCord Museum

p. 39 PHOTO #2: Photograph - *Looking toward river, bottom of Jacques Cartier Square, Montreal, QC, about 1886,* George Charles Arless, about 1886, 19th century, MP-0000.236.6 © McCord Museum

p. 39 PHOTO #3: Photograph - *Flood at Victoria Square, Montreal, about 1886,* George Charles Arless, about 1886, 19th century, MP-0000.236.5 © McCord Museum

p. 39 PHOTO #4: Photograph - *Custom House Square, Saint Paul Street, Montreal, QC, 1886,* George Charles Arless, 1886, 19th century, MP-0000.236.4 © McCord Museum

p. 41a: Photograph - *Highwater, Montreal harbour, QC, about 1870,* Alexander Henderson, about 1870, 19th century, MP-0000.1452.41 © McCord Museum

p. 41b: Photograph - *Flood, Chaboillez Square, Montreal, QC, about 1886,* George Charles Arless, about 1886, 19th century, MP-0000.236.9 © McCord Museum

p. 42-43: Photograph - *Flood, Bonaventure Depot, Montreal, QC, 1886,* George Charles Arless, 1886, 19th century, MP-0000.236.2 © McCord Museum

p. 44: Photograph - *Montreal wharves in winter, QC, 1865-75,* Alexander Henderson, 1865-1875, 19th century, MP-0000.1452.50 © McCord Museum

p. 48a: Photograph - *Montreal, looking south from tower of Notre Dame Church, QC, 1859,* William Notman (1826-91), 1900-1925, 20th century, VIEW-7048.0 © McCord Museum

p. 48b: Photograph - *Steamboat wharf, Montreal, QC, 1865,* William Notman (1826-1891), 1865, 19th century, I-16829.1 © McCord Museum

p. 49a: Photograph - *Harbour, Montreal, QC, 1884,* Wm. Notman & Son, 1884, 19th century, VIEW-1333.1 © McCord Museum

p. 49c: Photograph - *Harbour from C.P.R. elevator, Montreal, QC, about 1885,* Wm. Notman & Son, about 1885, 19th century, VIEW-1938 © McCord Museum

p. 49b: Photograph - *Steamers in Montreal harbour, QC, about 1910*, Wm. Notman & Son, about 1910, 20th century, VIEW-6582 © McCord Museum

p. 54bl: Photograph - *Harbour from examining warehouse, Montreal, QC, about 1890*, Wm. Notman & Son, about 1890, 19th century, VIEW-2230 © McCord Museum

p. 54br: Photograph - *Old shed, C. P. R.-London Line, Montreal harbour, QC, 1908*, Anonymous, 1908, 20th century, MP-1979.155.399 © McCord Museum

p. 60a: Photograph - *Entrance to Victoria Bridge, Montreal, QC, 1896*, Alfred Walter Roper, 1896, 19th century, MP-1977.76.8 © McCord Museum

p. 60-61b: Photograph - *Victoria Bridge, Montreal, QC, 1873*, William Notman (1826-1891), 1873, 19th century, I-84736 © McCord Museum

p. 61al: Print - *Centre tube in progress*, Anonymous, 1860, 19th century, M15934.28 © McCord Museum

p. 61cl: Print - *Monogram of Grand Trunk Railway Company*, John Henry Walker (1831-1899), 1850-1885, 19th century, M930.50.1.443 © McCord Museum

p. 61cr: Photograph - *Victoria Bridge, Montreal, QC, 1899 (?)*, Wm. Notman & Son, probably 1899, 19th century, VIEW-3249.A.1 © McCord Museum

p. 62l: Photograph - *Loading grain in sailboat "Lake Michigan", Montreal, QC, about 1878*, Notman & Sandham, probably 1878, 19th century, VIEW-812.1 © McCord Museum

p. 62r: Photograph - *Self-propelled floating grain loaders, Montreal harbour, QC, 1906*, Wm. Notman & Son, 1906, 20th century, VIEW-8749 © McCord Museum

p. 63l: Photograph - *Floating crane lifting marine leg, Montreal harbour, QC, 1909*, Anonymous, 1909, 20th century, MP-1979.155.171 © McCord Museum

p. 63r: Photograph - *Loading from floating elevators to ocean liners, Montreal, QC, about 1920*, Anonymous, about 1920, 20th century, MP-0000.25.204, © McCord Museum

p. 64-65: Photograph - *Aerial view of Montreal harbour, QC, about 1945*, Anonymous, about 1945, 20th century, MP-1985.47.1 © McCord Museum

p. 68: Photograph - *Shed's roofs, Montreal harbour, QC, about 1910*, Anonymous, about 1910, 20th century, MP-1979.155.141 © McCord Museum

p. 72ar: Photograph - *Elevators and sheds, Montreal harbour, QC, 1919-20*, Wm. Notman & Son, 1919-1920, 20th century, VIEW-18940.1 © McCord Museum

p. 72br: Photograph - *"Cornish Point" and "Admiral Cochrane", Montreal harbour, QC, 1920*, Wm. Notman & Son, 1920, 20th century, VIEW-19569 © McCord Museum

p. 75a: Photograph - *Harbour, Montreal, QC, about 1927*, Anonymous, about 1927, 20th century, MP-0000.25.205 © McCord Museum

p. 78l: Photograph - *Cold storage warehouse under construction, Montreal, QC, 1920*, Anonymous, 1920, 20th century, MP-1979.155.418 © McCord Museum

p. 78r: Photograph - *Cold storage plant in harbour, Montreal, QC, about 1925*, Anonymous, about 1925, 20th century, MP-0000.25.213 © McCord Museum

p. 82a: Photograph - *Montreal from Custom House looking east, QC, about 1878*, William Notman (1826-1891), 1930-1950, 20th century, VIEW-841.0 © McCord Museum

p. 82b: Photograph - *Harbour from Custom House, Montreal, QC, 1887-88*, Wm. Notman & Son, 1887-1888, 19th century, VIEW-1940 © McCord Museum

p. 84al: Photograph - *Harbour Commissioners, Montreal, QC, 1888*, Wm. Notman & Son, 1888, 19th century, II-88103 © McCord Museum

p. 85bl: Photograph - *J. W. Hopkins, Montreal, QC, 1864*, William Notman (1826-1891), 1864, 19th century, I-13130.1 © McCord Museum

p. 94al: Photograph - *Hon. John Young Monument, Montreal, QC, about 1913*, Wm. Notman & Son, about 1913, 20th century, VIEW-4993 © McCord Museum

p. 94c: Photograph - *Hon. John Young, Montreal, QC, 1862*, William Notman (1826-1891), 1862, 19th century, I-4160.1 © McCord Museum

p. 100bl: Photograph - *Loading wood on the S.S. "Turret Age," Montreal, QC, 1895*, Wm. Notman & Son, 1895, 19th century, II112707 © McCord Museum

p. 101a: Photograph - *Freight landed from S. S. "Corinthian", Montreal harbour, QC, 1900?*, Anonymous, 1900, 20th century, MP-1979.155.52 © McCord Museum

p. 102-103: Photograph - *Unloading S.S "Durham City", Montreal, QC, 1896*, Wm. Notman & Son, 1896, 19th century, II-116749 © McCord Museum

p. 108: Photograph - *Group of sailors, about 1880, copied for F. Scott in 1926*, Anonymous, 1926, 20th century, II-271216.0 © McCord Museum

p. 110l: Print - *Laying the Monumental stone, marking the graves of 6000 immigrants near Victoria Bridge*, 1860, 19th century, M15934.45 © McCord Museum

p. 111b: Photograph - *Group of refugees or immigrants on ship, 1907-14*, Martin Wolff, 1907-1914, 20th century, MP-1981.160.258 © McCord Museum

p. 115al: Print - *Joe Beef's Supplement. Third Edition. Joe Beef's Canteen No.4, 5 and 6, Common Street Montreal.*, John Henry Walker (1831-1899), about 1885, 19th century, M995X.5.35.4 © McCord Museum

p. 125a: Print - *Grand Finale of Fire-Works in Honor of the Prince of Wales and the Successful Completion of the Victoria Bridge, Montreal, Canada East.*, G. A. Lilliendahl, 1860, 19th century, M975.62.263.3 © McCord Museum

p. 127b: Photograph - *Wharves, Montreal harbour, QC, about 1870*, Alexander Henderson, about 1870, 19th century, MP-0000.1452.38 © McCord Museum

p. 128-129: Painting - *Skating on the harbour ice, Montreal, QC, 1850-60*, John Henry Walker (1831-1899), 1850-1860, 19th century, M330 © McCord Museum

p. 133b: Print - *A Race on the Ice - Bicycles v. Skates*, Anonymous, 1881, 19th century, M975.62.72 © McCord Museum

p. 140: Photograph - *Skating rink, Montreal harbour, QC, about 1870*, Alexander Henderson, about 1870, 19th century, MP-0000.1452.64 © McCord Museum

p. 157a: Print - *Montreal, 1843*, John Richard Coke Smyth, 1843, 19th century, M1308 © McCord Museum

p. 158: Photograph - *Big John and party shooting Lachine Rapids, near Montreal, QC, composite, 1878*, Notman & Sandham, 1878, 19th century, II-50718 © McCord Museum

p. 161a: Print - *View of Montreal From Saint Helens Island,* Robert Auchmuty Sproule (1799-1845), 1830, 19th century, M970.67.19 © McCord Museum

p. 161cl: Print - *Rapids of St. Lawrence,* John Richard Coke Smyth, 1840, 19th century, M989X.72.15 © McCord Museum

p. 161cr: Print - *Windmill Point, on the St. Lawrence River,* Kilburn, 1855, 19th century, M975.62.405 © McCord Museum

p. 162-163: Painting - *The Port of Montreal, 1830,* Robert Auchmuty Sproule (1799-1845), 1830, 19th century, M303 © McCord Museum

p. 164a: Print - *An East View of Montreal, in Canada,* Thomas Patten, 1762, 18th century, M19848 © McCord Museum

p. 164b: Print - *View of the Port of Montreal, 1841,* C. G. Crehen, 1841, 19th century, M3181 © McCord Museum

p. 165cl: Photograph - *Ships and wharves, Montreal harbour, QC, about 1870,* about 1870, 19th century, MP-0000.3217 © McCord Museum

p. 165b: Photograph - *Square-rigged chaland, near Montreal, QC, about 1915,* Anonymous, about 1915, 20th century, MP-1979.155.341 © McCord Museum

p. 168: Photograph - *Sail barges in basin, Montreal harbour, QC, 1897,* Alfred Walter Roper, 1897, 19th century, MP-1977.76.25 © McCord Museum

p. 170bl: Photograph - *Steamer "Corsican", Montreal, QC, about 1875,* William Notman (1826-1891), 1930-1950, 20th century, VIEW-6523.0 © McCord Museum

p. 170br: Photograph - *Steamer "Quebec", Montreal, QC, about 1885,* Wm. Notman & Son, about 1885, 19th century, VIEW-1531 © McCord Museum

p. 171l: Photograph - *H. M. S. "Talbot", Montreal harbour, QC, 1897,* Alfred Walter Roper, 1897, 19th century, MP-1977.76.33 © McCord Museum

p. 171ar: Photograph - *S.S. "Bavaria", Allan Line, Montreal, QC, 1899,* Wm. Notman & Son, 1899, 19th century, II-130022, © McCord Museum

p. 171cr: Photograph - *Harbour, Montreal, QC, about 1900,* Wm. Notman & Son, about 1900, 19th century or 20th century, VIEW-3148 © McCord Museum

p. 171br: Photograph - *S.S. "Noronic", Canada Steamships, Montreal, QC, about 1915,* copied ca.1920, Wm. Notman & Son, 1915-30, 20th century, VIEW-5546 © McCord Museum

p. 172-173: Print - *Montreal, 1892,* Anonymous, 1892, 19th century, M984.210 © McCord Museum

p. 174: Photograph - *Hugh Allan, Montreal, QC, 1864,* William Notman (1826-1891), 1864, 19th century, I-10826.1 © McCord Museum

p. 176: Photograph - *Harbour, Montreal, QC, 1889-90,* Wm. Notman & Son, 1889-1890, 19th century, VIEW-2232.1 © McCord Museum

p. 179b: Photograph - *Ice breaker, QC, about 1910,* Anonymous, about 1910, 20th century, MP-1979.155.29 © McCord Museum

p. 180b: Photograph - *Harbour Commissioners tug "St. Peter", St. Lawrence River, QC, 1910,* Anonymous, 1910, 20th century, MP-1979.155.271 © McCord Museum

p.181a: Photograph, glass lantern slide - *Tugboats in harbour, Montreal, QC, about 1930,* Anonymous, about 1930, 20th century, MP-0000.25.59 © McCord Museum

p.183b: Print - *Lachine Canal improvements, Montreal, 1877,* Eugene Haberer, 1877, 19th century, M20947 © McCord Museum

p. 184bl: Photograph - *S.S. "Turret Crown" at lock, Lachine Canal, Montreal, QC, 1895,* Wm. Notman & Son, 1895, 19th century, II-111871 © McCord Museum

p. 184bc: Photograph - *S.S. "Turret Crown" in Lachine Canal locks, Montreal, QC, 1895,* Wm. Notman & Son, 1895, 19th century, II-111873 © McCord Museum

p. 184br: Photograph - *S.S. "Turret Crown" in Lachine Canal, Montreal, QC, 1895,* Wm. Notman & Son, 1895, 19th century, II-111872 © McCord Museum

p. 186-187: Photograph - *Harbour view, from canal locks, Montreal, QC, about 1875,* William Notman (1826-1891), 1930-1950, 20th century, VIEW-958.0 © McCord Museum

p. 196c: Photograph - *Dredge No. 2 and tug, Dept. of Marine, QC, about 1910,* Anonymous, about 1910, 20th century, MP-1979.155.100 © McCord Museum

p. 198: Photograph - *Wharves of Montreal, QC, 1872,* William Notman (1826-1891), 1872, 19th century, I-77117.1 © McCord Museum

p. 203c: Print - *Design for corporate name of Richelieu and Ontario navigation company,* John Henry Walker (1831-99), 1850-1885, 19th century, M930.50.5.549 © McCord Museum

p. 208bl: Photograph - *Reconstructed caravels, 16th C. ships at dock, Montreal harbour, 1893,* Samuel H. N. Kennedy, 1893, 19th century, MP-0000.2386 © McCord Museum

Michelle Guitard
p. 84bl

Ministère de la Culture et des Communications du Québec
p. 156b

Montréal Longshoremen's Union (SCFP), Local 375
p. 100a, 101bl, br

Old Port of Montréal Corporation
p. 23r, 53, 58r, 73a, 75bl, 80, 81a, bl, 90l, 117bl, 125b, 135al, 143bl, 146, 147, 148c, b, 149ac, bl, br, 182, 184cr, cl, 185, 192, 193a, 202a, 203a, b, 205a, 208a, bc, br, 209ar, ac, al

Olivier Hanigan
p. 2-3, 4-5, 6-7, 8, 13, 14, 18-19, 20, 24, 25, 27br, 31b, 39bl, 45, 52b, 55bl, cr, br, 56br, 59br, 69, 71, 75br, 76, 77, 79bl, 81br, 83, 85br, 86bl, br, 87br, 88, 89, 91r, 92, 94b, 95, 99br, 109a, br, 115br, 117br, 120c, b, 121a, 123, 124a, 132b, 133a, 134a, c, 135ar, bl, 136ar, al, c, 137br, bl, 138ar, br, bl, 139ar, al, 141, 143br, 144-145, 148a, 150, 151, 152-153, 154, 157b, 169, 177, 181c, b, 188-189, 193c, b, 197, 199, 200-201, 204b, 205b, 206-207, 209b, 210-211, 214-215, 221, 222, 224

Patrice Lamoureux / Mattera Inc.
p. 90r, 91r, 118c, b, 119al, ar, 121br, bl

Paul Labelle
p. 130-131

Pauline Desjardins
p. 26-27a (drawing Pierre-Luc Ménard), 67 (except al), 73bc, 84r, 85a, c, 87l

Photothèque La Presse
p. 194

Pierre Girard
p. 155, 212

Port of Montréal Archives
p. 22-23l, 39al, 46-47, 52a, 55a, 56c, 57, 67al, 70br, 72l, 73ac, 74, 79al, ar, cr, br, 86a, 94ar, 96ar, b, 97, 98b, 99a, c, bl, 104bd, 106, 107, 111h, 178, 195, 196a, br, bl

The Gazette
p. 191b: Gerry Davidson, *The Montreal Star / The Gazette* (Montreal) / PA-163164

Bibliography

Anctil, Pierre. *Saint-Laurent: Montréal's Main.* Sillery: Septentrion, 2002.

Association québécoise pour le patrimoine industriel. *Montréal portuaire et ferroviaire. Proceedings of the 5th AQPI Conference, Montréal, May 8-9, 1992.* Montréal: Association québécoise pour le patrimoine industriel, November 1993.

Association québécoise pour le patrimoine industriel. *Le silo n° 5 du port de Montréal et son secteur : le passé, l'avenir. Proceedings of a study day organized by AQPI and Héritage Montréal.* Montréal: Association québécoise pour le patrimoine industriel, September 1998.

Bonin, R. "Le canal de Lachine sous le régime français." *Bulletin des recherches historiques* 42, no. 5: 265-299.

Bouchette, Joseph. *The British dominions in North America, or, A topographical and statistical description of the provinces of Lower and Upper Canada, New Brunswick, Nova Scotia, the Islands of Newfoundland, Prince Edward, and Cape Breton.* London: Longman, Rees, Orme, Brown, Green and Longman, 1832.

Brouillette, Benoît. "Le port de Montréal, hier et aujourd'hui." *Revue de géographie de Montréal* 21, no. 2 (1967): 95-234.

Camu, Pierre. *Le Saint-Laurent et les Grands Lacs au temps de la voile 1608-1850.* Montréal: Éditions Hurtubise HMH, Les Cahiers du Québec, Collection Géographie, 1996.

Camu, Pierre. *Le Saint-Laurent et les Grands Lacs au temps de la vapeur 1850-1950.* Montréal: Éditions Hurtubise HMH, Les Cahiers du Québec, Collection Géographie, 2005.

Canada Lands Company (Old Port of Montréal). *The Old Port of Montréal Public Consultation: Background Information Summary.* Montréal: Consultative Committee on the Old Port of Montréal, 1985.

Canada Lands Company (Old Port of Montréal). *The Old Port of Montréal Public Consultation: Final Report 1986.* Montréal: Consultative Committee on the Old Port of Montréal, 1986.

Cardinal Hardy et Associés, Peter Rose. *Plan directeur d'aménagement.* Montréal: Old Port of Montréal Corporation, October 1990.

Centre d'histoire de Montréal. "16. Sports et carnaval d'hiver à Montréal au XIXe siècle." [http://ville.montreal.qc.ca/portal/page?_pageid=2497,3090469&_dad=portal&_schema=PORTAL]

Chartré, Christine, and Paul Trépanier. "L'ancien poste de police du port de Montréal." Quebec City: The Federal Heritage Building Review Office, Canadian Heritage, Report 91-107, 1991.

Courcil, Sabine. "De l'évaluation de l'effet structurant d'un projet urbain à l'analyse des congruences entre stratégies d'acteurs : le réaménagement du Vieux-Port de Montréal." Ph.D. diss., Faculté de l'Aménagement, Université de Montréal, 2002.

Desjardins, Pauline. "From the Warehouses to the Canal by Rail ca. 1830, The Lachine Canal, Montréal, Québec." *Northeast Historical Archaeology* 28 (1999): 57-70.

Desjardins, Pauline. *L'organisation spatiale du Corridor du Canal de Lachine au XIXe siècle.* Quebec City: Association des Archéologues du Québec, Collection Mémoires de recherche 3, 2006.

Desjardins, Pauline, and Geneviève Duguay. *Pointe-à-Callière—From Ville-Marie to Montréal.* Sillery: Septentrion, 1993.

Desjardins, Pauline, and Louise Pothier. *Étude de potentiel archéologique du territoire du Vieux-Port de Montréal.* 5 vol. Montréal: Old Port of Montréal, 1989.

Desloges, Yvon, and Alain Gelly. *The Lachine Canal—Riding the Waves of Industrial and Urban Development 1860-1950.* Sillery: Septentrion, 2002.

Dubuc, Alfred. "Montréal et les débuts de la navigation à vapeur sur le Saint-Laurent." *Revue d'histoire économique et sociale* 45 (1967): 105-121.

Hallé, Jacqueline. "Analyse architecturale : Élévateur N° 5—Port de Montréal." Montréal: The Federal Heritage Building Review Office, Canadian Heritage, Report 95-87, 1995.

Hallé, Jacqueline. "Entrepôt frigorifique : Vieux-Port, Montréal, Québec." Montréal: The Federal Heritage Building Review Office, Canadian Heritage, Report 96-52, 1996.

Labelle, Ernest. *L'histoire de la police sur le port de Montréal sous le régime des Commissaires.* Montréal: Port of Montréal, 1980.

Labelle, Ernest. "Fresque historique du Port de Montréal." *L'Escale* (March-April 1985): 35-37.

Lefebvre, Christiane. "La tour de l'Horloge, Vieux-Port de Montréal." Montréal: The Federal Heritage Building Review Office, Canadian Heritage, Report 96-35, 1996.

Lelièvre, Francine, ed. *Montréal, by Bridge and Crossing.* Montréal: Pointe-à-Callière, Montréal Museum of Archaeology and History and Editions Nota bene, 1999.

Linteau, Paul-André. "Le développement du port de Montréal au début du XXe siècle." *Historical Papers / Communications historiques* (1972): 181-205.

Parks Canada, "Standards and Guidelines for the Conservation of Historic Places in Canada." Gatineau: Parks Canada, 2003. [http://www.pc.gc.ca/docs/pc/guide/nldclpc-sgchpc/index_e.asp]

Port of Montréal. *The Gold-Headed Cane.* Montréal: Port of Montréal, 1988.

Prévost, Robert. *Montréal—La folle entreprise, chronique d'une ville.* Montréal: Stanké, 1991.

Provencher, Jean. "McKiernan, Charles, known as Joe Beef." *Dictionary of Canadian Biography Online.* Toronto/ Quebec City: University of Toronto/Université Laval, 2003. [http://www.biographi.ca]

Richard, Jean-Jules. *Faites leur boire le fleuve.* Montréal: Cercle du Livre de France, 1970.

Robert, Jean-Claude. *Atlas historique de Montréal.* Montréal: Art Global/Libre Expression, 1994.

Société de développement de Montréal, Ville de Montréal, Ministère de la Culture et des Communications. *Old Montréal: History through Heritage.* Edited by Gilles Lauzon and Madeleine Forget. Montréal: Publications du Québec, 2004.

Société de développement de Montréal. "Le patrimoine du Vieux-Montréal en détail." Montréal: official website of Old Montréal, 2006. [http://vieux.montreal.qc.ca/inventaire/hall.htm]

Young, Brian J. and Gérald J.-J. Tulchinsky. "Sir Hugh ALLAN." *Dictionary of Canadian Biography Online.* Toronto/Quebec City: University of Toronto/Université Laval, 2003. [http://www.biographi.ca]

Acknowledgements

A work of this nature could not have seen the light of day without the support and collaboration of many people and organizations. I first want to thank the Old Port of Montréal Corporation and its president, Claude Benoit, for initiating this project and supporting the entire process. Thanks also to the Corporation's communications director, Lily Robert, and her team. I also want to express my very special thanks to Pierre Émond, former vice-president and chief executive officer of the Corporation, and to Pierre Beaudet, of Parks Canada, for having invited me in 1987 to lead the study examining the archaeological potential of the territory of the Old Port of Montréal and thus to dig into the historic strata of a captivating site.

At the Éditions de l'Homme, my thanks go to the editor, Erwan Leseul, who managed to navigate among the reefs inherent in the editorial adventure to bring this work safely into port; and to the vice-president (editing), Pierre Bourdon—who bears the same family name as the Jean Bourdon who drew what we believe to have been one of the first maps of Fort Ville-Marie!—, who also had faith in this project. Their staff also deserves all my thanks, especially Mélanie Sabourin, who obtained the copyrights to the illustrations and compiled the accompanying credits.

I want to underline as well that the craftsmanship and flavour of the book are also due to the graphics work of Patrice Saint-Amour of Éditions de l'Homme, the magnificent photos of Oliver Hanigan and Annick Poussart's close involvement in the writing of the text. All three enthusiastically helped me to present what is often highly technical information in a pleasant, coherent, visually accessible and clear way.

A number of photographers provided us with images of current activities on the quays of the Old Port of Montréal that underscore the transformation that has come about in the last twenty-five years. Let's not forget either all the photographers and illustrators that have over the centuries left an incomparable iconography of the port of Montréal. And we must give credit to the work carried out by archive facilities in preserving documents and images. Without them, we could not have compiled this never-before-published portrait of our past. Many archivists have guided me through vast collections, checking the accuracy of the captions and the quality of the images supplied. A special thanks to Denise Duguay, supervisor of document management for the Montréal Port Authority, who responded faithfully to all my documentary or iconographic research requests; to her predecessor Ernest Labelle, who very kindly replied to my many questions on the evolution of the port; and to Heather McNabb, of the Collection and Information Management Service of the McCord Museum of Canadian History, for the pictures taken from the Notman Photographic Archives. Thanks also to Carol Cloutier, Library and Archives Canada; to Gilles Lafontaine, City of Montréal, document and archives management; to the documentation technicians at the Bibliothèque et Archives nationales du Québec; and to Bruno Galland and Luc Requier of the ministère de la Culture et de la Communication, Archives nationales de France, for the surprising photograph of the Canadian pavilion in the shape of an elevator.

Others have generously supplied more specialized information, offered their stories or reread the texts or their translation, skilfully done by Barbara Sandilands. Thanks to Mario Blanchet and Denis Wolfe of the Montréal Longshoremen's Union (SCFP), Local 375; to Lise Bousquet, who shared with us her memories of childhood in the port and at the "Lunch" with her father, Joseph Alfred; to Gerry Burnett and Peter Burnett, for the information on James Russell; to Denis Carrier, who spared me many tedious hours of downloading by making available to me his banks of digital photos; to Luc Dumontier, Montréal Port Authority, for details on the Conveyor Tower; to David Hanna, of UQAM, for information on the subject of railway networks and for proofreading the English translation; to historian Paul-André Linteau, for reading the complete manuscript and for his invaluable suggestions; to my colleagues and friends Gisèle Piédalue, for her sound comments after having read the English translation, and Gilles Rousseau, for his explanations concerning the geomorphological characteristics of the St. Lawrence Plain and the distinctive features of navigation on the river.

Lastly, I want to thank those closest to me for their encouragement throughout the voyage.

PAULINE DESJARDINS

Table of contents

Printed in Canada at Quebecor World